Dirt

Witch

The Mud Home

By Atulya K Bingham

Dirt Witch
A MUDHOUSE BOOK

Cover photograph by Melissa Maples
ISBN:9781787232945

"I consider myself a person who is connected to nature, somebody who respects the Earth; this book has me walking through the world with all my senses opened," Emma Batchelor, *Phoenix Rises Poetry*.

"Entranced! Be inspired by one who's lived and breathed dirt." Kim Sui, *Get Rugged*.

"Reality meets fantasy, myth, dirt, and poetry. I'm hooked!" Jodie Harburt, author of the sustainable lifestyle blog *A multitude of Ones*.

"This is such a compelling book. It will make you want to abandon everything you know, move to the forest and commune with the trees and earth. A must read for anyone harboring desires of creating their own magical space," Luisa Lyons, actor and writer.

"Engaging and thought-provoking. The act of reading this seemed to affect me on a level beyond the words," Claire Raciborska, author of *Growing Wild and Free*.

For the incredible trees of our planet,
and to all those who hear them.

Dirt Witch

Introduction

These days I'm a natural builder and author, but it wasn't always that way. Once upon a time I didn't know how to bang a nail in. Once upon a time I was afraid of snakes and scorpions. In those days I was, like most of us moderns, completely disconnected from my wild side. Eight months camping alone on a Turkish hill without power or running water changed all that though. It changed *me*.

I think once you've heard the Earth speak and felt your wild woman or wild man flex their muscles, there's no going back. Because the world of concrete and plastic, flush toilets and deodorant, though convenient, lacks the elements we are deeply crave: Magic, fulfilment and life.

For those who have read *Mud Ball*, this is the prequel. It is a little different. A little weirder. *Dirt Witch* charts those eye-opening first months I hunkered alone in the dust before I built my house. It reveals what was happening to me psychologically and spiritually, and has been described by some as a parallel mud world. So it isn't simply a straight forerunner of *Mud Ball*, but something more multi-layered, something closer to ecopsychology.

I have written this book firstly because Grandmother Olive asked me to, and secondly because so many people over the years have questioned why I wasn't afraid up on Mud Mountain (sometimes I was), how I managed to remain alone (I never felt I was), and how I dealt with the various creatures and challenges I encountered. I don't feel I can answer those questions adequately without referring to another kind of reality, one some may think of as fantasy, but I personally perceive as the non-physical side of ourselves.

May anyone who reads this take what they can from it, and weave their own mud magic. Because this world needs Dirt Witches and Earth Wizards like it needs oxygen and sunlight. It needs wild men and women living living from their souls rather than their minds, and with conviction.

To download any of my free mud building guides, learn more about off-grid living, or to follow my current situation in the *Earth Whispering* blog, visit www.themudhome.com

3

Artwork by Catherine Stevenson

The Meeting

"You can't live up there alone! There's no water. No electricity. In a *tent*?"

Nilay's eyes were wide. Her hair was bound in a scarlet silk scarf and the tassels shook as she spoke. "Look, if it's come to that, we'll put you up until you get yourself back on your feet."

My friend was perched in a lilac armchair fastening a bead into an earring. I looked out and inhaled the view. The rocks were Mesozoic creatures poised above us. The pine forests were ancient worlds. It was beautiful. It was wild.

"I'm telling yer, I wouldn't do it, and I'm a guy!" said Evren. "'S not a good idea. What about the boar? Old Ramazan was taken to hospital when one hit him on his motorbike. Skewered him right in the thigh. And the snakes and scorpions? And how you gonna survive without water?" Nilay's husband fingered his thick moustache. I could see a few grey hairs appearing in it.

"I'll get a water connection. I've just got to speak to the chief. It's my land. At least I won't be paying rent!"

"Yeah, but what you gonna do till you get connected? *If* you get connected." Evren huffed, and stepped out from the shop and into the garden of dreadlocks, henna tattoos and hair wraps that comprised the campsite. He pulled out a leather wallet of tobacco from his back pocket as he went. "Nilay's right. Stay with us," he said, before walking off.

We were huddled inside a gorge on one of Turkey's most exquisite coastlines. I scanned the shop walls speckled with bracelets, necklaces and earrings. Nilay had created almost everything herself from stones, driftwood and other natural items she'd collected from the beach.

My friend tugged at the ashtray, and gently rested her cigarette in it. The corners of her eyes softened. "What happened to your yoga camp idea? You were so into it," she said.

I sat back in my chair and allowed a long sigh to escape. It hissed as it left my throat. Hatefully, I stared at the floorboards. My jaw bone became a rigid boundary.

Bringing my gaze to meet Nilay's, I whispered, "No. That's over. I'm done with being good and helping people. You know what? From now on I'm going to be a witch."

Nilay lowered herself back into her chair. She slowly raised both eyebrows. Then she roared with laughter. It was a full-bodied guffaw, and suited her as perfectly as her headscarf. "Oh Kerry!" she wheezed. Then she craned her neck around, "Evren! *Evreeeen!*" She called out in the direction of the bar. "Bring us some drinks. *Now!*"

Little did I know that penultimate evening as I washed down my plans with a margarita...little did I comprehend the strange world I was about to enter, nor what it would do to me. Because being a witch wasn't what I thought it was.

***

The very next morning, I was edging the car down the ragged track. It swerved right and left rollercoaster style. A small ravine fell away on one side. A forest rose on the other. The road slid sharply down, rocks pushing the wheels up like tough white fists. I pressed the brake.

This mutilated strip of dirt was the 'road' to my land; a 2500-square-metre plot with no power, no running water and definitely no house. It was this field that I was headed for now.

Pulling off, I parked under a pine branch. The limb belonged to a curled, dry dragon of a tree. It bristled green and black, hissing under the glare of the sun. Still in the driver's seat, I closed my eyes, pressing my thumb and forefinger against the bridge of my nose. This was madness. Yes, I'd probably look back on this moment and see it as the point I finally tripped off the edge.

I was almost forty years old and with nothing to show for it. At least nothing that would normally be considered important. No partner. No kids. No career.

I'd just sunk that well and truly. Now having reached a crescendo of desperation, I was going to pitch a tent halfway up a Turkish mountain, because I simply couldn't think what else to do.

After a minute or two of procrastination, I pushed the car door open and swung a leg out. It was the beginning of May. The Mediterranean sun was a straggle of hot fingers. They reached through the branches and clawed at the bonnet. The heat smote me. The forest was heavy with grasshoppers, and they throbbed against my eardrums. But what else was creeping about within that morass of untamed foliage? This was an alien place. A place I didn't belong. Assiduously I checked the ground for critters with stings or fangs, or both.

The boot creaked as I opened it. I hauled out the tent bag, and it struck the earth with a jangle. It was a $50 nylon steal I'd found in the bargain bucket at Carrefour, and I wondered how it would hold up. Next I dragged out the pick, spade, and rake I'd just bought. With a groan, I slung the tools onto one shoulder and gripped the tent in the other hand. Then down I went. In every meaning of the word.

You can't live up there alone. Even I wouldn't do it and I'm a guy.

The words were stones rattling down from a precipice where I had just lost my footing.

At the bottom of the hill, a small pathway veered to the right. It slipped through clusters of dog roses, fragile bonnets rocking as I passed. Then I drew sharply to a halt. Oh dear. Eyes popping, I sucked in a lungful of burning air. I was here. On my land. Unfortunately, it wasn't what I'd expected.

My lower lip wobbled a little as I scanned the slope. It was engulfed in thorns. They were huge, taller than me. Insects buzzed within the morass of stalks, as though the land were a machine whirring to life, a Frankenstein. Something cold and heavy lurched inside me, because everything had changed. The hill was no longer the

8

bucolic pasture I'd last seen in April. It was a hot, bristling wilderness. The only evidence of humankind was a small cottage the other side of a pomegranate orchard, and a sheeny row of polytunnels below. This was rural Turkey. And I was alone.

Gingerly, I picked my way through the tall stalks flinching at the possibility of vipers. I was terrified of snakes, just *terrified*. Staring at the huge thorn bushes – great monsters baring tough green claws – I started to feel nauseous. My mind became a city at rush hour. It flashed anxious thoughts at me like traffic signals. Had it really come to this? Bumming in a Turkish field?

And then it happened – the meeting that would alter my destiny within this patch of Mediterranean scrubland. The encounter that would change me. Forever.

"My land!"

I jumped. Swivelling about, I felt my heart punch into my throat. Good grief! Someone else was here!

"*My* land!"

I stood still within the dry grass, tent bag swinging in one hand, tool handles in the other, like hunter or prey, I couldn't be certain. Then I saw her. And I swallowed very slowly when I did. My epiglottis squeezed the saliva down, but only just.

There, right at the edge of the forest, was a woman. At least I *thought* it was a woman. She might have been an animal. Yet she was familiar. Too familiar. A character that had clawed her way out of a dream. The back of my neck prickled as I took her in. Her head was a nest of brown matted hair. She had black wolf eyes, and was brazenly bare-chested. I knew her from somewhere. *Where?*

As I stared onto my slope, the strange beast-woman began beating her chest. Somewhere far off in the distance, I heard the thud of a drum. It spoke a language I recognised, but didn't want to.

9

"My land!" She snarled again, even louder now. Then she stamped her naked feet on the earth and bared her teeth.

I gaped at the bright white fangs, appalled. The outer layers of my persona raised disapproving eyebrows. Deeper within, guerrillas of dread peeped out from grimy subconscious holes.

And then without warning, the beast-woman was gone. Vanished. Into the shadows of the forest. And I was left staring, tool heads protruding over my shoulder, feeling more than a little disturbed.

***

It took three trudges up the dusty red hill to transport my belongings onto my land. Long, hot peregrinations they were, along the edge of the fearsome forest. The pines creaked as I walked, their trunks coiled like bark-encased springs. My ears ached from acute listening. My eyes smarted.

On the final leg, I struggled metre by metre with two ten-litre water canisters. It was a punishment worthy of the Middle Ages, my arms gradually wrenched from their sockets. I stopped to rest a good ten times.

You can't live up there alone! There's no water. No electricity. In a tent?

The jackals of Nilay's words circled me, shoulders raised, heads lowered, hungry for the blood of my already-wavering conviction.

Once it was over, I sat under an olive tree and stared at my paltry heap of belongings: a tent, a kilim, a sleeping bag, a sponge mattress, sheets, a duvet, an icebox stuffed with food, a small suitcase of clothes, books, and a flowery toilet bag, all piled under the olive tree.

How well I remember that moment now. As I surveyed my pathetic hill of possessions, I thought it might be the end. But now I see, that's exactly what we *have* to think. That's the point we have to come to to risk it all, and to find the pieces of us we don't know exist. Because no one has ever transformed within the safe confines of the tried and true.

The sun inched past the first olive tree, and the streets of my mind filled up once again. There was a honking of horns as thoughts collided into each other.

Survival. Night coming! No house. Tent. Needs erecting. How much daylight? Shit!

I needed to get a move on. But the fact was, I didn't know where to start. How long would it take to create a camp? What exactly did such a thing entail? I hadn't a clue really, but clearing a square of dirt seemed like a good idea.

Glancing over at the jumble of poles and metal that was my tools, I debated which to use. To my unacquainted eye they were all ancient weapons. I'd used a pick and a rake once before in my life. A spade, on the other hand, had never graced my palm. Half-heartedly grabbing the thing, I stepped out of the shade and over to the edge of the grass.

The terrain was a chest-high rampart of yellow stalks with seed-stuffed ears that shook like rattles. They hissed as a short breath of air moved over them. It wasn't inspiring.

"Here goes," I called out to no one in particular. Then I pushed the handle toward the ground feeling as incapable as a person can.

There was a clunk and a clang. The handle quivered, jarring my arm. The spade head had dug in about half an inch. Lesson one didn't take long to learn. You can't dig with a spade in Mediterranean soil. It's fifty per cent stones. Cursing, I let the spade fall to one side.

I wandered back over to the tool pile, this time grabbing the pick. Immediately I grimaced. It was heavy. Everything was heavy. My life. The afternoon heat. These wretched tools all of which seemed designed for bears rather than people. How was I ever going to clear a space for my tent before dark?

Survival. Night coming! No house. Tent. Needs erecting. How much daylight? Shit!

The thoughts circulated the roads of my mind like lost fretting tourists. Meanwhile the air burned. The grass rustled. And the eyes of the forest looked on. Carefully wading through the shuddering stalks, I clutched the wooden pick handle in both hands, and lifted it a little. Then I let it strike the soil.

Poof! Dust leaked out of the ground as it puckered and loosened. So I raised the pick a little higher and swung again, only this time harder. It plunged into the earth dislodging more rocks and stones with a satisfying crunch.

"Aha! This is the way!" I shouted, enjoying the brief spurt of optimism.

I raised the pick a third time. Wham! The earth splintered, releasing a smell that was strangely delectable. Kneeling down, I ran my fingers through the soil, inhaling its aroma. Stones and pebbles fell through my fingers. They looked like nobbled, grey gems. Something inside the coffin of my chest flickered, an old cobweb-draped candle perhaps, or a penultimate matchstick.

The work began in earnest now. I hacked. I dug. I pulled at boulders with the pick, feeling them loosen like rotten teeth. I raked. I scratched. I hauled and cut. The grass began to pile up in a small, sweet-smelling stack. Rocks shifted into line. The sun rolled on, unconcerned. It notched up the hours like a fiery hand as it drew its invisible circle overhead.

And then my arms complained. They burned. And my legs began to tremble. My shoulders had fried in the sun. Though I wasn't unfit, I was utterly unused to outdoor manual labour, and my body was already screaming. As the light turned copper, and then violet, I quietly panicked. Evening stretched over the sky in a purple smoke, and I stared at the dirt gap in the grass still conspicuously devoid of a shelter.

It was then odd things began to take place. Things cities and standard educations and modern ethics don't prepare you for. Things you don't necessarily feel comfortable with...

"My land!"

It was a distant growl, but I heard it. My skin crawled, and my spine shrank into a brittle line.

"My *home!*"

The voice moved closer. I flung my head up and searched the twilight. The rocks pushed up from the soil like half-submerged tombstones. They were glowing an ethereal white. A slight breeze bothered the trees, and I shivered. A twittering cloud of birds pulsed and swirled overhead. The cloud morphed into a black arrow, and it plunged into my land before mushrooming into a large sphere and sinking within an oak tree. Something itched inside me, something very old, prehistoric even.

"Mine!"

I turned my gaze to the forest on my left. It was a tall wood of inky holes. Slowly my eyes widened as I watched a silhouette move out of one of them. Feeling for the rock beneath me, I held my breath. As the shape developed limbs and features, queasiness filled my belly, drip by cold clammy drip.

The beast-woman. She was back.

"Me no beast! Me *wild*," she boomed. The words banged slowly and heavily up the land like an aggravated diplodocus. Surreptitiously, I flicked my eyeballs left and right while holding my head and torso dead-still.

"Okay. You're wild. My mistake, Wild Woman," I muttered into the thickening air. And again I sensed the gangs of dread bunching up ready to ambush. It was a terror I couldn't see. A shadow I couldn't locate. As though I was harbouring a creature within me. Gestating an alien.

"Me from the *dirt!*" she growled. I could just about make her out now, striding in my direction, her incisors glowing like the stones.

"Right. I see. You're from the dirt," I repeated slowly. I rocked on my perch nervously. Heck! Night was almost here and there was a dirt primitive on the loose. I wondered what to do about it. I decided it might be best to strike up a conversation.

"Erm, well nice to meet you, Dirt Woman..."

13

Silence. I squinted and tried to spy movement in the forest, but all I could see was darkness. I battled on. "Er, you know this is your land...?"

Stalks rustled. An eerie trilling began, as grasshoppers and katydids ushered in the gloaming.

"Well, the thing is, property acquisition and ownership, that all came in with capitalism. It's all to do with ego you know. The Earth belongs to everyone."

"*My* land!" Suddenly her face appeared. It was so close to mine, I felt her breath on my face. It was hot and strong. Her eyes were arrow tips poised at my head. Her body was a bow, pulled back and ready to launch. I gulped.

"But...but don't you think it would be more evolved if we *shared* things?"

The Dirt Woman moved her lips, hacked up something ghastly in the back of her throat, and spat it out in front of me. "Pah!"

I blinked. Clearly reason wasn't going to get me very far up here. There were other powers at work. One of them was something called evening.

Turning from my wild new acquaintance, I noticed both the shadows and the light losing their definition as the planet teetered on the verge between day and night. There was a coolness, and a lull in the breeze, as though something somewhere was waiting. And then I felt it. It surged into me from nowhere. Boom!

Despite having grafted all afternoon, despite arriving on the land feeling like a failed hobo, for no good reason at all as far as I could see, I came alive. Energy was pulsing through me as though I'd been plugged into the national grid, which was impossible as I hadn't even spoken to Turkish Electric yet.

My senses opened like a set of venetian blinds. Everything came into focus. I forgot about the Dirt Woman and property rights. There were perhaps ten minutes of light left at most. I had to get the tent up. This was survival!

Leaping to my feet, I ran over to the olive trees and snatched the tent bag. Immediately I hurled the sack of poles and pegs on the floor, and set about erecting the thing. Unbelievably, within five minutes the dome was shape, and I was positioning the tent door in front of the view.

The air was thickening now as the light faded further. Night was after me, chomping at the bit to crush all into darkness. I thrust a peg into the dirt at each corner. There was no hammer. And that didn't matter. As the ground was mostly rocks and dust, it made for a rudimentary fastening, but I guessed my belongings would weigh the shelter down.

Running now, I fetched the mattress, duvet and pillows, and I hurled them inside. The rest of my belongings followed. Hurriedly I arranged everything. I pushed the suitcases of books into the dome corners for ballast, and made my 'bed'. Last of all, I found my headlamp and hung it from the apex of the tent.

It was then it fell like an almighty black club. Night. It was here. And that strange energy – the power of twilight – was gone. It was as though someone had yanked me out of the cosmic plug socket and thrown me on the floor in a straggly, useless heap. Fatigue clobbered me. I knew if I sat down, I'd never rise.

Kneeling in front of the water canister, I poured a little into a bowl. Next I cursorily washed my face, neck and torso. The rest of my body I left to its fate. Darkness was now all over me in a blinding, impeding sludge.

Stripping off my vest top, trousers and underwear, one by one I hurled the rank, dishevelled articles into a corner. Then I zipped the tent door shut, before flopping heavily onto the duvet-covered mattress. I was so tired I didn't stop to wonder where the Dirt Woman had vanished to. Or whether she had actually gone at all.

Home. This was now my home. A four-person tent perched on a lonesome hill. If I had known then what I know now...if I had known I'd still be on that slope five years on, what would I have done?

Probably nothing. I was too tired. Nothing existed in that pit of unconsciousness. Not the past, nor the future, not my failures, nor my age. Not even this peculiar new Dirt Woman character. My land had sucked out my marrow, and now it was digesting it.

Taiwanese Dreams

Jhubei, Taiwan (six months earlier)

It was a cold, heaterless December in Taiwan. I pulled a pair of biker's gloves over my hands and tucked my woollen scarf tighter. I'd punched out from the primary school where I worked an hour ago, and was now part of an erratic rill of scooters chasing the lights.

Threading my Yamaha Fuzzy through Jhubei's neon-decked downtown, I tucked my head under. The city was a clutter of urbanisation on the west coast of Taiwan. In fact, the entire coastline was one long chain of cuboid metropolises. They were linked by a network of asphalt belts; grey noodles that squirmed through the dripping rainforests, car lights sliding endlessly over them.

It was only Tuesday. Three long days of punch-in and punch-out loomed between me and the weekend. As I pulled up to the restaurant, I felt nausea curdle under my diaphragm. Tedium and burn-out stalked me in equal measure.

***

"I've had my fill of it. I frankly don't think I have it in me to keep doing this. I say we just go now." Seth was spooning red Thai curry onto his plate. He was a handsome young man with the refreshing trait of not being in the slightest bit aware of it.

"*Ja*, I really don't think I can bear to stay another six months either. There has to be a way to do this. There's always a way." Claire picked up her chopsticks and dug into the vibrant palette of her dinner plate. We were sitting outside despite the drizzle prodding at the chilly night air. Jhubei High Street was a swanky strip of nouveau commerce. As always, it wriggled with night-time crowds clutching shopping bags and children.

Claire and Seth were from South Africa. They were my flatmates. And all three of us taught Taiwanese kiddies in a school just up the road. I was here to pay back a debt. They were here to save money. Not that we were the only economic refugees on the island. In 2009 Taiwan was awash with Westerners scrambling from financial disaster in the wake of the recession. The comedy or tragedy (depending on how you looked at it) was they all had to become teachers. American construction engineers, Canadian musicians, unemployed South Africans, young North Americans staggering under ponderous student loans, and a string of dubious fellows who might well have been evading prison, all were fed into the mouth of Taiwan's behemothic English-teaching mincer. Many never made it out.

I say we just go now.

The words alone were dazzling, sparkling amulets in a machine-world of drudge and judicious obligation. A scooter whizzed past our table and rattled over a drain cover. It was too much. I was the oldest of the group by a long way, but plodding caution has never been my strong point.

"Yeah, to hell with it! Let's quit. Ha ha!" I jumped up and punched the air with my chopsticks, feeling two or three of the system's greasy plugs pop out of me there and then. Freedom surged in.

Our table seemed to light up, and the three of us expanded with a newfound lust for life. We chatted and whooped and patted ourselves on the back for being daring go-getters.

"My God! The Mystic Yurt is coming to life!" I whispered.

The Mystic Yurt was the brainchild of Claire, Seth and me. It was our escape plan, and it was elaborate. I had a plot of land in Turkey upon which we would build a spiritual centre. I was already a seasoned yoga teacher, all three of us were meditators and writers. Seth had just had a spiritual book published. What could go wrong?

I'd always dreamed of running a yoga centre. God only knows why. Really, now I look at it, it was the single biggest delusion of my life. All I recall is this: a few months after stumbling upon a yoga course in my hometown of Antalya, a lifetime of depression was miraculously cured, and I became something of an evangelist (and yes, Antalya actually finds itself on the road to Damascus, if you're walking from Europe at least). least).

So I qualified as a yoga teacher. Then I spent many years and plenty of money on yoga teaching first in the Lost City, and then further down the Turkish coast. I wanted the world to see the light, preferably while in downward dog. The trouble was, the world wasn't particularly interested. At least not enough to sustain me. I dread to think the amount of hard-earned cash I poured into yoga platforms over the years, not to mention the financially disastrous creation of a yoga camp in Fethiye. And the hours and hours of my time I gave and for which people would sniff sourly at me because I was charging $3 a session. I should have quit in the beginning, long before I bankrupted myself. But I was passionate, manic even. And that, I'm afraid, is my curse.

Now here I was sitting in a Thai restaurant on Jhubei High Street plotting another attempt. Originally, in the embryonic stages of the Mystic Yurt, the plan had been to graft in Taiwan until the summer, after which we'd have saved enough money to put in to the project. But like Sméagol's precious, the dream took a hold of us. It was a shiny, golden orb of meaning in an uninspiring winter of blackboards, staff meetings, and marking.

I hadn't even clambered completely out of debt! But that damp night in December when Claire, Seth, and I clunked beer bottles and tucked into our decisive Thai meal, it was but a detail. They both believed in me. Therefore, I believed in me. The energetic wheels of the yoga mission were turning again. Nay, they were spinning.

"If we hand in our notice now, we could leave by Chinese New Year, couldn't we?" Claire placed her chopsticks on the table. Three pairs of eyes glistened. The drizzle thickened but no one cared because the damp seemed to evaporate off our skin.

"Oh, just imagine! No more practice-book marking. *Ever!*" Taking a swig of beer, I wondered if I could even wait another day.

"Amazing, just the thought of it makes you feel better, eh?" said Seth.

We were jumpy now, so we pushed our chairs back and stood to pay the bill. As we walked into the brightly-lit restaurant, tables of local eyes turned surreptitiously in our direction. Because we were possessed by a light. The light of freedom. And it glowed.

***

And so two weeks later, much to the consternation of our supervisor, all three of us quit our jobs. By Chinese New Year in February, we were flying out of Taipei. And by April we had reconvened in Turkey. And that's when things started to go wrong.

First, we found out that the visa laws had changed, which meant Seth and Claire could only stay for ninety days. We couldn't get hold of licenses to drive motorbikes, and my mechanic couldn't seem to find me a car. And then I began to have second thoughts, because from nowhere a little existential panic had visited me. All of a sudden, since reaching Turkey, I'd woken up to the fact that my 2500-square-metre plot was my one last possession. That I was nearly forty, and very tired. And that there was another dream, one I had never really dared to go for, yelping in the night of my heart.

Not that I was the only one hesitating. As we grappled with the practicalities of our yoga camp – the cooking, the hosting, the dreaded guests and their endless requirements – it began to feel as though we didn't really want to run a centre. It felt more like we all just wanted to sit by ourselves, and be quiet.

***

Two weeks later the Mystic Yurt finally skidded into the dust. Claire and I were sitting with the cups and teapots set up, waiting for Seth. He walked in from a bedroom, and sat between us, a little heavily, I thought. The water was boiled. The cups were filled. Seth adjusted his mat and pushed a bunch of hair behind his ears.

"I have something to say."

Claire and I fixed our eyes on him and waited.

"I don't want to do it," he said, and then slumped back from the relief of the confession. Claire and I both exhaled deeply. Everyone sat still for a moment. The room seemed to fall in on itself from the retraction of effort, as though it had been our willpower holding up the walls.

"You know what? Neither do I," I said, admiring the man's courage to speak the truth, when I had so obviously failed.

Seth shrugged. We both looked at Claire. She was sitting cross-legged with a red and blue shawl around her shoulders. She blinked. "I feel a little relieved," she said. "I mean I could have gone through with it. But..."

"I want to go home," said Seth. "I just want to go home." He hugged his knees and rested his chin on the caps.

I nodded, because I completely understood what he meant. Home. I just wanted to go home too. Wherever that was.

So that was the end of the Mystic Yurt. The end of yoga centres, and alternative communities. The end of life purposes and flashy dreams and do-gooding. I finally comprehended. That dream was not for me. Was I bitter? Very.

The Crone

As graveyards went, the Yapraklı one was beautiful; a small enclosure bordered by a stone wall holding five or six old olive trees and a handful of gravestones poking out of the earth at odd angles. The cemetery was perched on the top of a mountain that looked out over an endless expanse of jutting peaks and blue sky. The dead had an inspiring view. They also had a free water supply, which was why I was here.

"Damn!" The water splashed my boots and I felt my right foot turn cool. I turned off the tap in the wall by the cemetery gate. Once I'd screwed the lid on the plastic water container, I hauled it to the open door of my car. Grunting, I shoved it beside the other five bottles I had already filled.

"Ah, I won't have to do this for much longer," I muttered to myself. "Just until I get a water connection." And I slammed the car door.

I had no idea at the time just how intimately I'd get to know that graveyard, nor how I'd remember each tiny limescale mark on that tap. Had I been able to stare into those water bottles and see my aqua-starved future, I'd probably have cried.

Despite her twenty years of service, my Turkish Fiat didn't look or feel her age. She was gold and black, with a roof rack and a splendid new LPG tank custom built into the boot. The motor company had optimistically branded this line of Fiats "Sahin", or "Buzzard" in English, but to see the raptor in this car model required a fair stretch of imagination. She neither flew, nor soared, nor attacked. The Fiat Sahin was a plodder. And that's fine. Nothing wrong with a good, stable plod, if you ask me.

My Sahin chomped on the harsh contours like a Land Rover, humming merrily as she swung round the bends of my mountain lane. And this was why I decided to try and nudge her all the way to the bottom of the hill to save me that infernal walk. It was a preposterous gradient. But everything seemed preposterous at that moment, so I gripped the wheel and tried my luck.

The car lurched and rocked, water bottles slurping behind me. Dust billowed out from the chassis as my Fiat chewed on the road. Once we hit the sharp drop-away, the wheels skidded slightly. We veered to the right, and then to the left. Pulling to a halt at the base of the incline, I turned off the ignition and exhaled contentedly. The mid-afternoon sun bore through the trees scattering the forest floor with golden spots.

It was my second day as a tent-dweller, and I'd spent the morning in the nearest town shopping for supplies. Easing the car door open, I grabbed two bags from the passenger seat. I also eyed the brand-new wheelbarrow wedged onto the back seat between the water tanks. With its spotless cobalt paint and its virgin tyres it looked like the new kid at school.

Bags in hand, I trotted onto my land. The dry grass and dust itched my nose. A swallowtail butterfly drifted in front of me. Its wings flapped lazily, two filigreed cream ears pierced blue at the lobes. As I picked my way along the small path that was now forming at the back of the land, I sensed I was entering another world.

The three olive trees on the right of the plot rose into view. How different they were, these three trees. One was sturdy and lush with a miraculously straight trunk for an olive. Another was curvaceous, limbs curling gracefully about her. The third was a scraggy mess.

It was afternoon. The trees flung distended shadows onto the ground, and they merged to form a lagoon of shade. I gravitated toward it, relishing the idea of sitting peacefully for an hour. It was not to be.

"Yoo hoo!"

I dropped my bags. Who in hell was *that*? I didn't want to see anyone. I'd already decided that this was my private place. My secret world.

There was a rustling from behind the largest olive tree. I watched in dismay as a dwarfish figure stepped out from the shadows. It was the woman who lived at the other side of the pomegranate orchard that bordered my land. We'd met once before. With her baggy, speckled şalwar trousers and her green headscarf, she was a wrinkled, sun-tanned gnome.

"Eh, and how are you getting on? I've been wondering about you, I have. Heard a car, so I thought I'd just pop by and say 'allo." She threw me a hearty grin. It was so utterly devoid of agenda that I wavered. The crone pushed further onto my land.

"How did you get in?" I asked, a little perturbed.

"Oh I climbed over the fence," the little lady replied with a nonchalance that was alarming. Fence. *My* fence. The border between *my* world and hers. Somewhere feet started thudding on the earth and drums began banging again. I could see I'd have to put a stop to this fence-hurdling lark at the soonest opportunity. Give people an inch and they take a mile. Before you know where you are they're stealing your oranges and nicking your hand tools.

"I'm sorry, what was your name again?"

"Dudu," the wizened mouth expelled proudly. She looked up and caught sight of my tent. Both her eyebrows lifted into her headscarf. "Ooh, well would you look at *that*! You've set up a nice little camp, haven't you? Clever girl! *Maşallah Maşallah!*"

I scratched my head. Firstly, I was a good twenty years away from anything resembling a girl. And then, *Maşallah! Maşallah* is an amulet of a word. In Turkey, whenever a local sees something beautiful, well-made or enviable, they expel a conclusive *Maşallah*. This is to ward off any subconscious jealousy they might be emitting that could harm the other person. It's the verbal version of the evil eye. I wrinkled my nose in bemusement, because I couldn't imagine that even in the darkest, most covetous nooks of Dudu's brain she would be jealous of my Carrefour tent.

Dudu sighed and then began scanning the place for somewhere to sit. I hoped she wouldn't find anywhere. I had things to do. She ambled over to a large white boulder and plonked herself on it, her legs wide apart in the typical style of a rural woman. I knew I should offer her a drink. It's extremely rude not to take care of your guests in

26

Turkey. I was bitter. I didn't like people anymore. So I was extremely rude.

"I don't have water. I'm sorry I can't offer you a drink."

Dudu batted the hint from the conversation like an inconsequential fly.

"Ooh, I know what it's like. We were the same when we first moved here. No water connection in those days. My husband, God rest his soul, would come down here, right here, to this ditch. It fills up with fresh water in winter and you can drink from it, you know."

Ah, now *this* was news. Water? There was potentially water up here?

Dudu scanned my land, and her face abruptly crumpled. "Oof! You want to get rid of all this grass, my girl. Pronto! And all these bushes. Pah! They'll be snakes and scorpions and heaven only knows what in there. Clear it. Cut it. Burn it. Get rid of it! Horrible dirty stuff."

I stared at my plot a little offended. "I think I quite like the brambles. They're protecting me," I said.

The little old lady's mouth puckered. "I tell you, you want to cut them all down. Brambles, grass, bushes, trees. Clear this space right up. Clean it."

Trees? Cut trees?

"Well it was very nice of you to visit, Dudu. Now, I've got quite a lot to do before dark..." I stepped out toward my tent.

"You put poison round your tent didn't you? Sulphur. The yellow stuff. That'll burn the skin off those snakes. They won't bother you then," Dudu called after me.

I blinked. Snakes. Once upon a time I'd suffered such a phobia, I couldn't even look at a photograph without verging on a cardiac arrest. At the sight of a live one, I'd turn white, shudder and emit a series of non-descript gurgles, before charging off at a speed that might just have qualified me for the national 100-metres squad. In saner moments, I would try to access that same acceleration when running for the bus, but it never worked. Snake speed was a phenomenon unto itself.

By 2011 though, having spent fifteen years residing in a snake-filled country, I'd become a little more familiar with the legless and scaly. I'd progressed from the phobic, to the plain, straight scared.

"Have you seen lots of snakes, Dudu?" I posed the question pleadingly.

"Hundreds!" Dudu replied, eyelids stretching to reveal plenty of white. "All over the place, they are. Big black ones as thick as your wrist! And those fat-headed ones with the diamonds. Ooh, you want to be careful of those. They'll kill you before the ambulance gets here!"

A long slow gulp made its way from the back of my tongue to my stomach.

Leaping from the rock, Dudu hoisted up her şalwars and adjusted her cardigan. "Ooh, I'm so happy to have a neighbour! I've been waiting and waiting for you," she said, almost breathlessly. "I was frightened up here all by myself, especially at night." Her eyes stretched into owlish circles when she said the word 'night'. "You know, since my husband passed away, God rest his soul, I don't like it one little bit. You never know *what's* wandering about in the dark, do you? I shut myself in my house, lock that door and stay right there until dawn, I do." She shuddered. Then she fixed her eyes on me, and looked me slowly up and down. "Aren't you *scared?*" she whispered.

"Oh no," I lied, shrugging the question from the back of the conversation like an itchy sweater. Scared? I was anxious about nightfall already. Yesterday I'd dropped unconscious, but tonight?

"I love being alone. That's why I'm here, to be *alone,*" I added, emphasising the word alone by raising my index finger of my right hand into a number one.

Dudu turned, paying not the slightest attention, and made for the gap in the trees. "You can pop over whenever you like for water," she said. "How *lovely*! Now we can be friends. You need friends up here, my girl. Everyone does."

I groaned, albeit quietly. Then the little shawled figure slid behind the olive trees and disappeared into the leafy wilderness of the pomegranates.

***

Two hours later, I was arranging the reed mat I'd just bought in front of the tent. I'd cleared more grass around my dome now too, so there was now space to walk around it. The reed mat was my balcony. And a new solar lantern was charging. As I stood back and admired my new camp, I was slapped by a splash of pride.

It was then that I noticed something. The grass smelt different. The temperature had dropped a little too. I looked up and noticed the wild shrubs at the bottom of the land had turned a peculiar shade of green. The trees became dark bird-collecting hands. Turning my head to the west, I watched the last sliver of sun disappear. Twilight. It was here.

And once again I felt it. That power. Only this time I paid more attention. Life force was wafting out of the earth like an exotic perfume. Or perhaps it was seeping in from the air. Whichever it was, it was stretching into my muscles. I was alive and awake.

Twilight is a power pocket. This was one of the first natural secrets I was initiated into by my land. You can lounge about and do nothing all day, it matters little, as long as when the light starts to fade you are ready. Because you will achieve more in the hour before dark, than you will in the rest of the day. The System with its cumbersome nine-to-five workday policy understands nothing of this. An hour is not a reliable measurement for productivity, for each hour of the day has a different value and a different energetic potential. Better The System doesn't know. Better we keep these secrets to ourselves.

Scanning my tiny camp, I wondered how I should use Twilight Power while it lasted. I decided to create a small rock terrace.

Rushing over to the centre of the plateau, I plucked (and now it felt like plucking, not hauling or dragging) the rocks from the surrounding earth and resettled them in the 'wall'. I was filled by such a sense of well-being and purpose. The ruggedness of the elements nourished my very soul. The dirt was no longer worthless brown crud, but the living skin of a massive ancient being.

Finally I managed to yank myself away from the wall. It was hard to stop, it really was. I was possessed.

I sat upon my new step and stared into the darkening vale. The forest at the edges was turning into something from a fairy tale, a place where Little Red Riding Hood met wolves, and Hansel and Gretel stumbled upon frightening hags.

It was then I sensed something else. An awful realisation crept over me. It turned my flesh into cold lumps. Someone was sitting next to me. And by the smell of her she hadn't washed for a while.

"*My* land!" The words were growled softly this time. But the essence of them was no less potent.

How had she managed to appear just like that out of nowhere, like some (very dirty) apparition? A plum of dread pushed up my throat. I said nothing. Sliding my eyes to the right, I studied Dirt Woman: her body hair, her sweat, her muscles. I felt into my fear, trying to understand it. Because whenever I looked at this woman, I encountered the nasty sensation she was family, that she was closer to me than I was currently prepared to admit.

Dusk was a murky smoke now, but I managed to gather myself. Dirt Woman was underdressed, had too many teeth, and desperately needed to be acquainted with a hairbrush. But I had to get to the bottom of her.

"Look, if you're going to stalk me, you'd better explain a thing or two. I'm scared enough as it is."

"Stalk? What is *stalk*?" The darkness had now deepened to the extent I could only make out Dirt Woman's eyes and teeth. But at least she was speaking to me. This was a development.

"Erm, it's kind of like hunting I suppose."

A few incisors appeared. "Me no hunt you. Me no like your taste!" And with that she coughed up a good egg cup-ful of saliva and deposited it noisily on the ground between us. I baulked, and then raised my eyes to the sky. She didn't notice. It was too dark.

"I help you. You lost in forest," she said.

"I'm not *lost*. Well, not exactly." It was a flimsy protest. I shuffled on the protruding edges of the rock, before admitting, "Actually, I *am* lost. Completely."

Two rows of teeth became perfectly visible. "You no be afraid. I your friend." Dirt Woman whacked me on the shoulder. It was a slap so hard, I was winded.

"Thanks," I squeezed out weakly, bracing myself for further contact. "That's made me feel *so* much better. Who needs enemies, eh?" But my more ancient side had already leapt to her feet. Half-chimpanzee, half-antelope, she sprang over the stones and galloped through the dry grass. Briefly, I wondered about her bare-foot policy. The last thing I heard was a whoop, before silence and darkness prevailed.

I looked up. The North Star had appeared. One by one the lights of Alakır Bay flicked on in the distance, as if mirroring the stars in the sky. And I sat there a while, pondering on reality, sanity, and the psychological theory of Carl Jung.

I wanted to be a witch, because witches are dangerous, rebellious, and don't care what people think. They can access powers that the regular world doesn't understand, powers that override brute strength and money, powers that create and destroy. But perhaps my ideas of witchery had also been doctored. Perhaps becoming a real witch meant going back further than I had realised, delving into wilder, dirtier terrain. Perhaps it meant connecting with something more elemental. Something unashamedly raw and true.

Night Life

The stars were popping through the ink of night like faraway eyes. Venus had winked at me long ago. The three studs of Orion's Belt gleamed overhead. I was sitting on my first earthwork, a raggedy, rickety one-layer 'wall'. The air had turned cool, and I rubbed the tops of my arms.

Standing up from the wall, I stretched. Then I turned to enter my tent, but I couldn't see it. Night was here. There was no moon. Not a flicker of light except the stars overhead. There were no more olive trees, no mountains, no glimmer of polytunnel plastic from the land below. Just an enormous, all-pervading blackness.

You never know what's wandering about in the dark, do you? I shut myself in my house, lock the door, and stay right there until dawn.

Dudu's words filled my head. My heart pushed into my throat. But I had nowhere to shut myself other than my tent. And I was hungry. Somehow I was going to have to deal with the wild night, the strange noises, the terrifying threat of the invisible and therefore imagined. Scrunching up my shoulders, I tried to stop thinking about it.

First I needed my headlamp. Its designated position was the top of the tent where it hung with the solar lantern. Grabbing its ribbed band, I stretched it over my head and pressed the button.

As I stood up, my beam of light swept across the top of my plot. The land became a surrealist canvas under its thin ray; the grass surrounding the tent was now bleached of colour, and the thistles scattered within it jutted up forming erratic, angular sculptures. I raised the headlamp a little. It caught the periphery behind the grass. The leaves of an ancient olive tree picked up some strands of light. Two thick pine trunks reared out of the darkness as my plucky bar of light hit the ridges of their bark. Beyond that was the fearsome forest. But it was invisible, subsumed into the void of night. I shuddered at the thought of it, and all that might be in there.

I considered the wild boar that were probably wandering amidst the pines. The snakes, the weasels and stoats, porcupines and foxes. Slugs of fear began to slide into me. They slithered through my eyes, down my throat, and into my guts, releasing a cold trail of terror as they descended.

There was nothing to be done. I had to deal with the night. One by one, I pulled the flapping, disbanding parts of my reason together and focused. And what better to focus on than food? My headlamp beam sank onto the icebox. The water canister was squatting next to it along with a plastic washing-up bowl. I sighed. Now I comprehended the point of a kitchen. I had nowhere to wash-up dishes, nowhere to store them either, and nowhere to prepare food. No table. Nowhere to sit. I found myself thinking about the first humans. How had it all begun? All this food preparation, the need for utensils, fires, and the like. And what would it be like to try and live without them?

Ten minutes later, I was perched gingerly on a rock trying my best not to think about scorpions. My dinner was a cheese and tomato sandwich. Hungry as I was, the bread stuck in my mouth, a masticated ball of starch. I chewed and chewed feeling immensely dissatisfied. Tomorrow, I'd have to come up with something else, something involving a pot and a fire.

Eventually I returned to my tent. Digging around in one of the crates, I found some toiletries: olive oil soap, a toothbrush, a comb. And then I wondered where to wash. Heck! That was another thing I needed, a bathroom! I mean, it wasn't sanitary to just crap and spit all around my tent.

Adjusting the torch beam, I scanned the darkness for a spot. The twisting edges of the forest were illuminated. I gulped, poured some water from the canister into a small water bottle, then bucked up and separated myself from my little camp. How I trembled as I picked my way through the ghostly sea of grass to the east side of the land near the forest! My heart swelled to the size of a melon. It pounded and bumped in my chest so vigorously I could hardly breathe, and the two-minute walk became one prolonged flinch.

Once I reached the forest edge, I hurriedly pulled out my soap. Crouching over a rock, I did the best I could with a litre of water. Then, as fast as I could manage, I peed, and washed my hands. My frantic bathroom routine had almost reached its conclusion. I was in the middle of brushing my teeth, when I heard an eerie cry. It floated out from the forest in mournful puffs. And if the sound was anything to go by, it was dressed in a white sheet.

Oooh. Wooh.

I froze, toothbrush in mouth. My senses sharpened themselves into five needle points of discernment. This was a sensation I was going to experience frequently in the coming months. The popping open of perception. The heightened awareness. The adrenalin surging primed for fight or flight.

The cry drew closer. It drifted morbidly through the treetops, arcing over my plot. I had no strategy. No plan. I simply hunched rigid, toothbrush sticking out of my mouth, ears so attentive I half expected them to have grown fur and be poking out of the top of my head. This wasn't the adrenalin-provoked stress city folk experience when they are given a parking ticket, nor the crushing worry over some intangible figures on a bank balance, nor the pent-up frustration of dealing with a tax form. No. This was different. It was present tense only. It was pure, undiluted terror.

The moaning moved so close, I knew it was only feet away from me. Flicking my head up, the beam of my lamp caught something white overhead. A plume. The cry moved from the west to the east side of the land. Finally I realised. It was an owl.

I flopped in relief. An *owl*? Fear turned to wonder. Ooh, an owl! Just imagine that, I had my very own owl! As if sensing my pleasure, the bird settled in a clump of trees nearby. It hooted and hooted, clearly calling someone. Pulling the toothbrush out of my mouth, I saw exactly whom. For there, buried beneath the clutter of modern convenience, beneath the suncream and deodorant, I saw Dirt Woman. And I was somewhat mortified to notice she was rolling on the ground, clutching her stomach in hysterics.

"Hey! Where the hell were you when I needed you a second ago? I was terrified!"

"Me here. You no see. Why you so scaredy-waredy?" My dirtier side stopped laughing and wiped her eyes.

"Scaredy-waredy? I've no idea where you picked up your English, but I'm pretty sure no one from the Cro-magnon era says *scaredy waredy*."

"Me no from there. Me from *here*," she stated somewhat cryptically.

I swilled some water round my mouth and spat a toothpasty splatter onto the rocks. Dirt Woman gawked at me, and then sniffed. The inhalations were short and focused like a dog's. Next, she crouched, stuck her nose in the dust, and inhaled noisily along the ground. Following this odour trail, she reached my feet. Her nose sniffed up my leg, over my torso to my mouth, as though someone had stuck a line of cocaine on me.

The bridge of Dirt Woman's nose wrinkled, and she eyed me suspiciously. "Me no like your smell."

"Me no like yours either," I retorted, before sucking in some air and correcting myself. "I mean, *I* don't like yours. Anyway, I'm off to bed. I don't like it out here. You said you were my friend, but you don't act much like one." I felt myself scowling.

Dirt Woman's features softened. She moved forward.

"All we are your friend." She opened her palm and held it toward the forest. The owl chose this moment to coo, and then alighted from his branch and moved further into the trees. Scrunching up the same hand, Dirt Woman stepped toward me and banged her breastbone once. "We are *family*!" she said, chin and chest jutting out.

"Yeees. That was sort of what I was worried about," I murmured.

I caught Dirt Woman's eye. "This is *home*," she said quietly, and stretched her hand out to fondle a leaf. She pulled the leaf to her cheek and closed her eyes smiling. *Home*. I had to admit, even the sound of it made me feel safer. Warmer.

My dirt 'friend' released the leaf and turned. There was no farewell. She simply padded away. Or did she stalk a little? I almost chortled when I spied her ruffling her hair.

This is home. My heartbeat slowed to its usual inaudible rhythm, and as it did, my thoughts whirred back to life. When had we moderns become so disconnected? Where had the great separation begun? I looked up and stared into the great dome of the night sky. It was a canopy of stars. A black velvet marquee. It was so deep, and stretched so unfathomably far I was awed by it. Now that my fear was abating, I began to look properly at the cosmic night. It didn't feel distant, no. It was intimate and warm, each star a bright eye watching over me, an intergalactic retina. Reaching for the leaf the dirt woman had stroked, I felt my something inside my heart stir, something I'd thought I'd lost, or forgotten I'd ever possessed.

Belonging. This is perhaps one of the greatest ailments of the modern human. We spend our lives chasing relationships and jobs simply to feel we have a place. To feel connected. Home. We contort ourselves into the most painful shapes for social acceptance, because we think if society approves of us we will belong. But it never works. Far below the surface, there is an all-pervading unease. Because the society to which we're trying so hard to belong, has itself come unmoored, long ago. It is very much lost at sea. We are tethering ourselves to a wayward vessel heading for a cyclone.

Torch in hand, I returned to my balcony. Unhurried now, I pulled off my shoes. Finally, I squeezed through the tent hatch, zipped it up and crawled into my sleeping bag. To this day, I can still feel the silky nylon on my legs, and the delicious cosiness of that tent. Its innards were illuminated by the solar lantern turning the space into a protean blue cave. It was like snuggling up inside a jellyfish.

Outside, I could hear the shrill lullaby of the cicadas. As I gaped at the stars through the hatch, something else drifted over to the mesh. A tiny light. How odd! It glowed like a fairy cigarette. Raising my head a little, I wondered what on Earth it was. It looked alive. Soon another light joined it. Then another. Until finally there was a veritable crowd of will-o'-wisps hovering.

I blinked. Peered closer. And then I saw. Fireflies! Throngs of them. Pushing myself up on my elbow, I stared in fascination as these minute glowing beings began to play, or huddle, or whatever it was they were doing. The orange dots twirled and circled and danced all about my door, as though choreographed. I held my breath, eyelids pried back, determined not to miss a thing. The mosquito netting of the door became a living fabric of enchantment. My eyes prickled. The only way I can describe how I felt as I watched this magical display, is blessed.

I know there were probably many reasons that the fireflies gravitated to my door, but as I lay there in my blue dome in the middle of an overgrown field, it was hard not to believe the display was put on just for me, Mother Nature's idea of a housewarming.

As my lids grew heavier, I pondered on all our gadgets of entertainment, our phones and tablets and TVs. All this paraphernalia, all this techno-distraction. Not one had ever made me feel the way I did as I watched the fireflies or heard the owl. Awe. Mystery. Connection. Even a dash of love. It's the fabric of life itself, something so intimately us and simultaneously so far beyond us that we feel neither danger nor boredom. Life on Earth *is* a miracle.

And perhaps Dirt Woman was right. It was also home.

Survival

We have been taught that we have to struggle to survive. It is such a deeply-ingrained belief, it has become its own miserable self-fulfilling prophecy. Most nature documentaries continue projecting this survival struggle story (and that's what it is, a story, a narrative, a fiction created by a human mind) onto the natural world. Trees struggle for light, animals suffer tough existences from birth to death merely trying to eke out food and avoid predators. Life is one long horror, and if it's not horror, it's drudge. I was brought up on such documentaries. And on the face of it, it appears true. Work work work. And then you die, apparently.

But what if work and play are the same? What if your survival is the most fulfilling thing you're likely to do, so much so that you can't wait to get stuck into it? What if the physical activities you engage in for your shelter and food happen by some miracle to rid you of negative emotions and fill you with enthusiasm? What *then*? What if a tree's most exciting mission is to search out sunlight? What if it loves the quest?

"Oh, anthropomorphic fool," the documentary narrator shakes his head condescendingly. *"Trees don't love."* Well, in that case, they don't struggle or suffer either. These are human ways of assessing life. We're always gluing our own attributes and emotions onto the natural world. Well, we would. There's no other way for us to conceptualise it.

Yet as the years have passed, I've noticed something: as my experience of natural living evolves, so do my projections onto nature. And as my projections change, inexplicably so does nature itself. What do I mean by that? Well, nature starts behaving differently. It's exciting. Magical even. And unfashionably unscientific.

Back in May 2011, none of these insights had occurred to me. I had too much else to think about. I was still a newbie. Mother Nature was burrowing into my pores, but She hadn't upended my long-standing belief systems yet. My mind was still an office block stuffed with insurance brokers, bankers and scammy pension salespeople.

***

"Yoo hoo!" The pomegranates on the other side of my fence began to rustle. A quiet but decisive whine left my lips. *Dudu.* She was back. And it wasn't even nine o'clock! I sat up to see her clambering over the metal wire.

"I've brought you a couple of aubergines. And here's a bottle of water. Thought you might need them. What are you eating?" Dudu hitched up her şalwars a little and sat next to me.

"Cheese sandwiches," I replied mournfully.

"Cheese sandwiches? That's not much of a breakfast, is it, girl? Where are you keeping the cheese? It's getting hot up here now and it's only going to get worse. Ooh, summer will be so fiery, it'll boil our blood and our brains into soup!"

I nodded. "I'm keeping my food over there in the icebox," I said leaning back against the trunk of the olive.

Dudu screwed her eyes up and studied me. It was a look I'd come to know well over the next few weeks. She wrinkled her nose, then her forehead. "Why don't you get someone to help for goodness' sake? I've got a neighbour who's always looking for a bit of extra work. He'll be only too happy to lend a hand. You'll have to pay him, but he's cheap. A good sort."

I sighed. "Because I don't like people, Dudu. I'm sick of them. I just want to be by myself." Then I sat up. "I want to do this alone. It's going to be my special space, the only place in the world that's mine, that no one *ever* can take away from me. It's going to be *my place.*" I banged my hand down on the ground between us.

Dudu raised an eyebrow and moved her lips in and out. "I see," she said fiddling with the knots on her headscarf. "It's gonna take you a pretty while to get through that grass on the top there, isn't it though? It'll be growing back before you've got to the end of it."

I didn't say anything.

"And it's full of snakes, and tailies."

"Tailies?"

"Yes, you know." She curled her finger into a hook. "They've got a tail like this. Hurts something awful when they sting you. Ooh, one got me on the foot some years back. I'll never forget it!"

"Ah, scorpion. You mean scorpion."

"Well, yes, *some* people call them scorpions," she sniffed. "But here in the village we all call them tailies."

I chuckled. "Tailies. Okay, I've learned a new word."

Dudu stood up. Even when she drew herself to her full height she only reached my shoulder. And I am hardly tall myself. "Thanks," I said. "Thanks for the aubergines."

"And you'll be needing some ice for that icebox too, eh? You can stick some in my freezer if you like." With that, Dudu swung a dumpy leg over the fence. Then she turned and vanished into the pomegranates.

Dismally, I looked at the handful of white bread remaining in my hand. Then I lobbed it over the wall and let it flounder upon the slope below. My food situation was dire. But one thing I *had* arranged was a small gas tank upon which I could boil water. A pot of filter coffee sat beside me, and I was relishing every drop of it. As I supped the black brew, the caffeine invigorated my mind, and I started to consider my survival.

Currently, I was perched upon a flimsy economic raft. It would probably ferry me across the banks of summer, but after that? Life was going to be cheap up here, but certainly not free. I had to run the car. I still had to eat, and if it was one more cheese sandwich I'd vomit.

Placing my mug on the earth, I gazed over at my tent languishing under the sun. The small figures on my mobile showed 9:06, but the top of the land was already soaked in heat. We were still in May. I knew by late June all activity would be hopeless as the Mediterranean temperatures would start angling for 40 degrees Celsius. Clearly, I had to erect some shade, or both my tent and my belongings would be steamed to a pulp. Yet more urgent still was a bathroom. And even more pressing than that was a kitchen. I began to twitch as the panic filled my throat. There was so much to do!

The lights flicked on in the factory of my mind. Thoughts shunted along mechanical conveyors. They were stamped and punched into squares, before speeding down chutes, and processed into plans. Finally, my pulse calmed as the first 'to-do' list dropped into my head. The kitchen area with a wash rack. I'd finish that today.

Was it me or did the pine branches in the forest rustle extra vigorously, as though they were laughing? And did the jay in the myrtle bushes cackle? Did the great olive tree shake a little, dropping a cluster of dried olive pits? Because the kitchen was my first lesson that nothing, *nothing*, is ever done in a day. And no construction, be it a house or a washing-up rack, will ever be completed as quickly as you assume it will be.

Abandoning my coffee cup, I made for my tent. The sun was now zesty, smiting the land with firm, deft strokes. I donned a baseball cap and sunglasses, then surveyed the west side of my canvas. But here's the thing with building. You can't just *make* something. Because one job inevitably begets five more.

I saw immediately that before I could do anything, more grass needed clearing. Another small terrace had to be made. Only after that would I reach the wash rack. A weighty puff of air was pushed slowly from my lower abdomen and out of my nostrils. Grumbling, I headed toward the pick and the rake.

***

Three furiously hot and sweaty hours later, I was stretched out under the olive tree moaning like an injured footballer. My little terrace was complete. But that was all. No wash rack. No other hint of kitchen life. Just a space, empty save the dust and the bugs.

It was now midday, and I decided to rest for an hour until the sun had weakened a little. Closing my eyes, I let my back and hips sink into the oasis of dirt. The crickets had revved themselves up, and the olive tree was humming with them. But everything else was still. There was no breeze. No birdsong. My mind found a space to wander in. It was like a stray dog in a busy train station. It paced this way and that, trying to find its bearings.

What are you doing up here? Seriously! You're going to be forty in six months, and you're wasting time in a desiccated field making a place to wash your dishes? Get a job! You need a job. No one survives without a job.

The whirring of the crickets grew rhythmic. A light breeze had picked up. It rustled the leaves. And then calm stole over me, like a cool, freshly-laundered bed sheet. As I lay there, the tangle of self-analysis began to ease itself apart, as though the very earth was unknotting my worries. A tear rolled down one cheek and then the other. All the while the olive looked down on me. I stared at the ridges in the tree's bark. It was a beautiful tree, and seemed to disseminate that grace, so that the air and soil around it smiled. The more I looked at the tree, the more certain I became. It was watching me. *She* was watching me.

The future evaporated. The present expanded. And I remembered. I was here. Alive. Healthy. With or without a stupid job.

***

An hour later I was awakened by a scratching noise. Hoisting myself up on one elbow, I looked up. Then I groaned. There, digging her toes into my freshly-raked kitchen space was Dirt Woman. She was butt-naked, breasts jangling proudly. Interlocking her fingers, she placed the bridge of her hands over her forehead, and raised her eyes in my direction. The matted entity that was her hair shook. Once again a chill crawled between my shoulder blades. I still hadn't quite got used to her.

"What is it?" she said, lowering her arms and pointing at the ground. A bemused line stretched along her brow.

"It's going to be a kitchen. Then I can cook spaghetti and wash my dishes."

The look I received was as blank as the deposits section of my bank account.

"I don't gnaw on bones," I added. It was a snarky defence and it didn't go unnoticed. Her eyebrows drew together. They were two furry fences of perturbation. "Me too. I no eat much bone."

My lower lip slid away from the upper. I ran my eyes up and down the dirt woman's physique. She wasn't big, in fact she was skinny. But the muscles rippled on her arms, thighs and midriff in tiny, ribbed bulges. "You're a vegetarian?" I asked, eyebrows pushing toward my hairline in disbelief.

"Me find food. This home good. Food all over. Why I kill my friend for eat?"

"But I thought, you know, you had one of those paleo-diet things going."

"Paleeeooo," Dirt Woman repeated, her tongue inspecting each vowel carefully. Then she skewered me with a stare so pointed, I couldn't even wriggle my way out of it. "Who tell you me eat bone?"

"I don't know. I thought it was common knowledge. Hunter-gatherer. A bit of hunt. A bit of gather."

"Much gather, little bit hunt[1]. This home forest very friendly. I am killing animal only in special time."

---

1 . Just as dietary trends change from month to month, so do ideas about what our ancestors were really eating. There can be little doubt, however, that 'developed' nations eat far more meat than their ancestors ever did. In the past archaeologists have over-emphasized the role of meat due to bones found at burial sites, however because plant remains degrade quickly, they would be unlikely to turn up in a dig. Recent research points to the fact that ancient humans actually had a more diverse diet than we do today, and ate an abundance of plants and herbs. **"Ancient Leftovers Show the Real Paleo Diet was a Veggie Feast"** Colin Barras, *The New Scientist*, December 2016. After living on my land for five years, this felt obvious to me. It would of course depend greatly on climate, but fruits and nuts are so easy to harvest

"Well there's something we have in common then. Hallelujah for that!"

Dirt Woman's eyes rolled to the upper right-hand corners of each socket, while her forehead crumpled. "Me no see you gather," she said after a moment's thought.

"Oh I do. It involves a wallet and a car. I call it shopping."

My naked cousin shook her head unconvinced. "That no gather. Gather is...special. Gather is like..." Once again her black eyes moved backwards searching for the word. "M...m...magic."

"Magic?" I repeated. Gathering was magic? I had no idea what she meant, but I liked the word 'magic'. Something tingled inside when she said it.

My landmate scratched between her dreads, eyebrows lifting before returning to the patch of dirt I'd cleared. "Why you fire food?" she asked, and bored her big toe into the dirt once more.

"You mean cook it? Erm...because that's what we do in our culture."

"Cul-chuure." The word was uttered thoughtfully.

I was now standing next to her, peering at her tanned flesh. Her skin was as smooth and firm as polished teak. Health and strength were coming off her like heat. "What do you eat then, if you don't cook and don't hunt?" I asked.

"Me eat nut, and brown pod, and berry and leaf and grass and seed and round fruit and... many thing I eat."

"Okay, let's get specific. What did you eat today?"

"Five brown pod. Some eye nut. Yellow flower seed."

My face muscles contorted in confusion. Eye nut? What *did* she mean? Observing my bafflement, Dirt Woman promptly turned and galloped across the plateau into the

---

compared to the effort of hunting. And in pre-agricultural human society there would have been a far greater abundance of plant edibles than there is today, when most of our forests and the wealth of fruits, greens and seeds within them have been cleared for livestock, or mono-crop agriculture.

forest. The speed with which she crossed the land was awe-inspiring. She was like an oiled brown leopard.

It didn't take long for her to return. She sprinted over to me clutching a handful of dry bits and pieces. When the brown twigs of her fingers uncurled, I saw carobs, almonds and sunflower seeds. Ah, almond was eye nut in her world, because of the shape I supposed.

"And this was it? Your breakfast and lunch?"

"Brown pod very good. You try."

"I know what they're like. Not that great. It's like chomping on a dry twig but sweeter. Anyway, where'd you get the carob? It's not the season."

"I keep in special place."

"Ah. You stored it, squirrel-style. Good call. But seriously, this would *never* fill me up. I need more energy. A few carbs, or an egg, you know?"

"Why you need energy? You no run. You no climb tree. You use noisy wheel machine." She flicked her head in the direction of the car.

"Well I'm digging...and making things like this kitchen," I said, pointing to the glaringly empty square of dirt.

Dirt Woman blinked. She was silent for a moment, three grooves stretching into her brow. She flexed her lips in and out, and wiggled her eyebrows. Finally, the result of her pondering was made known.

"You make kitchen for cook. You cook for eat. You eat much for energy for make kitchen..." Here she hesitated. Her black wolf eyes scanned me as though I was a complete lunatic. "This no good..." she continued. "I eat brown pod. I no cook. I no make kitchen. I sleep in tree and talk with animal. This good." And she opened her mouth and struck me with her trademark, tooth-filled grin.

I paused. Then I chewed the inside of my bottom lip for a moment. I felt an itch on the side of my mouth and lifted my index finger to scratch it. The tarmac on the roads of my mind was empty. Not a thought vehicle was to be seen. And it was then I spied it; the smallest of

47

green shoots pushing through the asphalt. But before it could take a hold, a truck of resistance roared out of nowhere and flattened it.

"No! I can't live like you. I just *can't*. I don't even think my digestive system functions like yours. Anyway, why are we standing here frying under the sun? Let's go sit under the shade of the olive tree."

And it was at this juncture something rather odd happened. Dirt Woman glanced once at the tree and shrank a little. She took a step backwards, then shook her head adamantly. "Me no go there."

"Why? I *love* that tree. It's got a great energy. I think it loves me."

But Dirt Woman was still retreating. I was dumbfounded. "Hey, what's wrong? Why don't you like the tree?"

My friend from the dirt pursed her lips and remained taciturn. Now I was intrigued. "Is there something in it?"

"Many thing in it."

"*Many things?*" Suddenly an awful thought occurred to me. "Oh no, there's not a snake, is there?"

Dirt Woman hunched her shoulders. Then she paced quickly off, past my tent. Without so much as a goodbye, she raced through the grass, before disappearing hurriedly into the caliginous holes between the trees.

I stared after her. Then I stared back at the great olive. Her branches were a fountain. Healthy green leaves frothed out of her with such vibrancy, I could sense the power from ten metres away. How old was she? I wondered. At least fifty, she had to be. If ever there was an example of the patient tenacity of life, it's the tree. Day by day, month by month, year by year, trees grow. Slowly. Steadily. Relentlessly. Bark thickening. Branches extending. New foliage bursting forth.

Staring harder at the olive tree, I suddenly sensed that while I thought I understood survival, I actually didn't. Because I didn't understand life. How it arises. How it sustains itself. Really, I didn't understand.

***

Afternoon was here. The sky was a sea. Tranquil. Azure. And the sun was a golden ship steaming pointedly across it. There wasn't so much as a crest of cirrus. All was blue. And light. As though the world were cut out from coloured glass.

Had there been anyone up in the sea-sky, and had they peered through that blue brine, they would have glimpsed a magnified version of me trying to make a wash rack. Which would have been entertaining. Because until that bright afternoon in May, I can honestly say I hadn't even put a shelf up. In all my forty years, I had never wallpapered or sanded or hammered a nail into anything, and the last time I'd wired a plug was for the electrician's badge in the Brownies.

This might explain, at least in part, why the wash rack became a major engineering project. All I had to go on, as I considered the options for creating such a thing, was a rack I'd made when I was ten years old on a Girl Guides' camp. As far as I could remember, it involved lashing together a bunch of sticks. Hmm, string. I needed string.

I didn't have any string. Nor did I have any nails. Nor a hammer. I wondered what to do.

Standing next to my tent, I absently stared out at the view. It was magnificent. The valley was one enormous dip in the Earth that poured out to the sea. I loved the feeling that I was at the top of that funnel gazing through pine forests and hills to the open water.

Funnel.

Valley.

Dip in the Earth.

An idea was tentatively scratching its way out of the dust. It threw one hand over, and then another, before heaving itself out of the dirt and sprawling into view. I gaped at it. Was this a plan? Aha.

Quickly, I scanned the area for the pick. It was laying on the ground by the tent. I grabbed it and moved about three metres from the canvas. Then I hacked a hole into the ground. It took about ten minutes because I still wasn't efficient at hacking.

Once I'd dug out a small valley, I wandered to the forest edge on the west side of the land. Frantically, I began collecting sticks about the width my finger. When my arms were laden, I returned to my hole. Laying the sticks next to each other over the hole, I created a type of rack placing a large rock at each end to stop the twigs rolling away. And what do you know? I had a wash rack.

If the sea-sky people above had still been watching, they would have wondered why a grin stretched from one of my ears to the other. For me, this was a breakthrough. I'd made something. Something useful. A wash thing. Out of nothing but twigs. *Nothing but twigs!*

My grin didn't disappear. I stood up and surveyed my work, the satisfaction sitting large and plump inside me. A brand-new player had just run onto the pitch of survival. And she didn't need money or a job. This was radical. It could change *everything*. As I mooned over the rack (and I spent a good half hour admiring it), I was so proud of myself, I decided to take myself out to dinner.

***

"You know, if you need any help up there, some of our boys could lend a hand, couldn't they, Evren? *Evreeen!*"

Evren swivelled round on his heel, beer in hand. "What?"

"Our boys could help Kerry for a day or two, couldn't they?" Nilay said through the thread between her teeth. She was tying a knot in one end of it and fastening a hook.

"We've got half a dozen lads here sitting on their arses till mid-June," said Evren. "Take 'em. I'm sick of looking at them." He raised the brown bottle of beer and took a deep swig. "Whatcha need doing then?"

"Actually, one thing I really need and don't know how to make is a big shade for the tent."

"Ah the lads don't know that kinda stuff. Well, I could come up with them I 'spose and show you. They can do the donkey work, and I'll just put it together."

"I'd love it if you did. Then I'll know how to do it next time," I moved forward on my chair, animated.

Evren raised a thick brown eyebrow, but remained silent.

"Yes, make sure you do it before the 15th of June though, because that's when the students break up, and then we'll need them, won't we, Evren?"

But Evren was already out of the shop on his way to get another beer.

Nilay sat back and lowered the driftwood necklace she'd just completed. Then she studied me. Her eyes were as polished as her stones. "You know what? I've had a brilliant idea," she said. "Why don't you teach yoga here in Café Cactus? We've plenty of space behind the campsite." She pushed her chair back and held up the necklace. Then she walked to the side of the shop and hung it on a hook.

"Really? You think it's quiet enough?" I sipped a glass of wine, sagging a little in disbelief at the way yoga teaching refused to leave me.

"I shall make sure it's quiet." Nilay crossed her arms over her ample bosom and threw the bar a ferocious look. "Oh, I'd *love* it! Yes, at last! This is what I've always wanted, yoga and t'ai chi and things."

"You mean Café Cactus Wellness," I said. We both snickered.

"Well, what are you going to live on otherwise?" Nilay stood up and wandered to the front of the shop. She was dressed in an olive green pair of şalwars and a tight black vest top. "We'll make a sign and put it right *here*." She pointed out to the roadside.

A car passed churning the air into a dusty smog in its wake. The pine trees on the roadside reared up with ophidian menace, trunks throwing green heads high in the sky. All around the valley rocks and crags and mountainsides pushed inward like closing gates, their rutted grey faces as implacable as a board of hard-nosed businessmen.

"Okay then," I let the words dribble out of me, incredulous that this was happening yet again. "I'll buy some cheap kilims and just flatten an area. Where do you think I can teach?"

"Oh, the orange garden, or even behind the orange garden. There's a beautiful spot no one ever goes to. Come, let me show you."

I exhaled. It was one prolonged puff of anxiety leaving my being. Yet some of the air remained stuck in the bottom of my lungs, lurking. Because I had already turned more than a little witch-like. I wasn't a white witch, nor even a black one, though. *My* witch was a mucky tinge of brown.

Nevertheless, it was decided. Over the next two weeks I'd clear a space at the back for yoga and teach throughout the summer. That would keep me financially afloat. It seemed like a plan. But then many things had seemed like plans up until now. If I'd known I was only going to teach one lesson before this one went up in smoke as well, I might have felt less assured.

The Tree that Whispered

"Don't you get lonely?" they ask. Everyone asks it. Because people have forgotten how to be alone. The word 'alone' doesn't mean isolated. It means all one. Complete. And how can you be complete, if you don't know who you really are?

There is a consensus in the modern world that personalities are nice, orderly, singular entities. We are one person, with one set of beliefs, one set of abilities, one set of likes and dislikes. And this is convenient. It makes us predictable, reliable, and wonderfully easy to pigeon-hole. It's also completely and utterly wrong. We are not one person (if indeed we are a person at all). We draw upon a range of personalities, role models and archetypes to create ourselves. Some of them might not be human.

But it takes silence to plumb our depths and retrieve the lost parts of ourselves. It takes patience and fortitude to sit with our shadows long enough to own them. Yet what gifts they clutch in their misshapen hands when they are finally allowed into light. Into the great sun of our selves.

***

I blinked. Then I gasped. I had just woken up and was prostrate in my sleeping bag, head facing the mesh of the tent. The sky was streaked with pink fire. Moses mountain was blushing rose. The birds were chirping and trilling with such infectious excitement, it made me laugh. The scene was so intensely beautiful, it was impossible just to roll over and sleep. I had to see more of it. Before it vanished.

Pushing the sleeping bag down, I yanked out my legs and slid toward the door. It was cool at that time in the morning, so I threw on a sweater. Then I opened the hatch and fell into the day.

Standing in front of my tent, I surveyed my land. The slope was now rippling gold with the sun rising over the peaks. Suddenly, such a fire of love ripped through my chest, I had to contract my throat. It hit me. This was my queendom! My home. My place goddamn it! *My Place.*

The wild grass shone as the sun bounced off it. The pines exploded in light. That such beauty could be bestowed upon me seemed incredible. I was back in Eden. I had never been thrown out. How had I ever been so confused?

Then, out from the forest, who should come bounding but the dirt woman? She strutted over the top of the land like a bare-chested rooster. When she reached the centre, the first ray of sun caught her hair. She opened her mouth and roared.

I flinched and cast her a weak smile, not really sure if I was pleased to see her. She was so brash. *I hope no one's watching,* I thought.

Was it me, or did the forest and the grass retract ever so slightly? Dirt Woman spun in my direction, matted locks of hair flicking over her shoulders. She patted her chest with her palm. "I am *real*," she growled, before turning her head and staring at me. "Why you afraid of neighbours' thinking?" she said, and promptly broke wind. "Why you afraid of your *culchure?*"

I stared sheepishly at my hiking boots, noticing a new hole appearing by the right toe.

Dirt Woman walked up to me and looked me up and down, the corners of her nostrils widening in frustration. "You be real! If you no real, you no living." She shook her head. Then she turned, and loped off into the forest. I gaped after her, nonplussed.

Just as twilight holds secret powers, so does dawn. And dawn is so often missed, either in the haste to reach a job on time, or in sleep. Unlike dusk, dawn is not so much about power, but about well-being. There is a reason the birds are euphoric and the sky shouts for joy. If dawn is both seen and savoured, it grants the observer both morale and meaning.

I breathed deeply. Turning from the view, I spied my new wash rack. For the umpteenth time, I admired it, a wave of satisfaction suffusing me as I did. It was hilarious, for it was no more than a hole with some sticks balanced over it. It was then I noticed I was excited. Very excited. It was the kind of excitement that grabbed my legs and arms and began moving them frantically back and forward. I turned to my little camp and looked it over. I wanted to make something else. *Now.*

Gripping my chin between my thumb and fingers, I pondered on what I needed most. As the sun pushed over the lower trees, the answer rose. Shade. I needed shade. Perhaps Evren would come and do it, perhaps he wouldn't. In the meantime, both my tent and I were frying.

I now had a small tool collection mounting behind my canvas dome. It was an open heap of metal and wooden handles. Picking through it, I found some gardening gloves. So I pulled them on and made for the forest.

As I wandered into the shadows, the dry leaves crackled. Spiky twigs pulled at my arms and hair. Vines throttled the gaps. It was another world in there, with its own rules, and I shuddered a little. Dirt Woman lived in here somewhere, but where? Was she perched in one of the trees? Or sleeping in a hole? Treading carefully, I scanned the earth for some thick branches. The plan was to wedge them into the ground around the tent and attach something over the top of them. This, I hoped, would create a small shade for my terrace.

***

An hour later my struts were laying in a heap by the side of the tent. By now the sun was a torpedo scudding directly toward my land. I pulled my cap down and braced myself against the heat.

Turning the branches over in my hands, I saw they were warped and bent, and not in any way standard posts. I wondered how to make them stand up independently. At that time I knew nothing of banging nails in and creating a self-supporting structure. All I knew was digging, and I wasn't particularly competent at that. But knowing always seems better than not knowing, thus I trotted over to my tool store and grabbed the pick.

56

Soon enough, I had clawed out a hole in the soil and stuck one of the recently gathered 'posts' in it. But it was far from secure. When I placed a hand on it and pushed it, the strut fell clean away. It was almost noon now. The heat was bearing down. Impatience began to rise like bile. I didn't know how to secure the post.

"Oh, for fuck's sake!" I shouted at the wonky branch, before throwing the pick on the ground in a huff. In an instant my good humour evaporated. I had no training or knowledge for the task in hand. Suddenly the whole endeavour looked like a waste of time.

Walking to my olive tree, I sat down heavily letting my spine collapse against the trunk. Then I extended my legs and crossed them at the ankle. In the inactivity and peace of the olive's shade, the clatter of my mind became louder. It was a juggernaut of noise and it ploughed through the countryside of my being, leaving clouds of dust in its wake. I was cross. I felt incompetent and incapable. I didn't know what I was doing. How could I have thought I'd make a shade? I'd got too far ahead of myself, that's what. Absently picking up a handful of shrivelled olives that no one had ever bothered to pick, I began lobbing them into the grass.

Yet the trunk of the olive tree was stalwart. Calm. The cicadas paused. The air grew thick and still. I closed my eyes and let my head drop back. One by one, the thoughts careering along the roads of my brain ground to a standstill. As my mind's highways grew less frantic, random memories found space to move. And it was then I sensed it. The tree. It was...well, it felt as though it was reaching out for me.

I twisted my neck round to look at the olive. Then I pressed my hands onto her fat trunk. The bark was warm, as though encasing the heart of the tree. I could feel the life moving through it, and it was beautiful. Potent. Strong.

I've always loved olive trees. They inspire a great respect in me. According to fossil findings, the olive has been around for a very long time, originating in the

Italian and eastern Mediterranean between 20 and 40 million years ago. They are incredible survivors and bountiful givers despite the aridity of their lands. Their fruit are eaten or pressed to create oil. This oil is then used not only for cuisine, but in soaps, and as a skin balm. Olive wood is durable and strong, and beautiful to carve. It's an evergreen tree too, providing shade in summer and wind protection in winter. What a tree!

Yet I was about to learn, these external functions comprised only one dimension of the tree's capacities. There were other mysteries. Other secrets. But I'd have to change my approach if I wanted to discover them, because it wasn't a head game, nor a strategy. The only way I was going to understand the power of life was to join with it, and allow it to communicate with me. To move into me.

You can't understand life by killing it, which ought to be obvious, but apparently still isn't in laboratories the world over. True discovery is not about dissecting and disembowelling, and arguing theories. It's an action that belongs to the heart and swirls like the rivers and the clouds. It requires trust and letting go. And it's going to be the make or break for our species in the years to come.

For me, it all began with this tree. The tree I would call Grandmother Olive.

The branches overhead rustled slightly. I remembered Dirt Woman, and her peculiar reaction. Staring up into the boughs, I wondered again what had provoked it. And this was when I first saw it. Or did I feel it? Or smell it? Something was raining down from the leafy canopy, or suffusing from it. A smoke? An essence? A chemical? This old olive tree was emitting something...something like a spell.

And quite suddenly, just like Alice, I found myself falling down a rabbit hole.

The dry branches of Grandmother Olive shuddered slightly. My attention shifted into another gear. Finally, I sensed a presence. Someone was here. And only now did I see her. Or rather hear her.

"My *dear* Earth-child, you don't need to work so hard. You are part of my family. The shade will happen on time. Everything always does once the seed is planted."

I pulled my knees up to my chest, and buried my head in my arms. The warmth of Grandmother Olive enveloped me. I lifted my face, rested my chin on my knees, and did something a little weird, something that might have qualified me for a spot of analysis had an urban modern been observing. I began talking to the tree.

"But how can it happen if I don't *work*?" I whined, shuffling in the dirt, a frustrated big kid.

"It's not about work. It's about beauty and adventure. It's a game! When you feel *that,* everything happens effortlessly. And when that feeling disappears, then it's the moment to take a break, and let time and light step in."

The words – or were they thoughts? – shone inside me like extra-terrestrial beads. Time and light? What did it mean? And what was I doing talking to a tree? Even worse, I was *hearing* a tree speak. Trees don't speak. They don't have mouths and cerebral cortexes and synapses and things. They don't think, and therefore they *don't* speak.

I turned my head away and flicked another olive stone into the grass, bemusement welling up inside me. Because it didn't make sense. If these were thoughts, then where had they come from? The ideas weren't anything I recognised as mine. I wasn't even sure I understood them.

"Have a nap, dear. It will *all* be sorted out for you." The tree was dripping beauty and peace all over me, and I started to fear I might drown in it. Would I fall in to that vaporous hole in which tree-huggers, vegans, and other sentimental bunny-loving types lurk? You know, that foggy den of empathy and emotion generally denigrated by intellectuals and rationals. That place where eyes roll, smiles turn smug, and no one takes you seriously any more.

It didn't occur to me to question why sensitivity and empathy have been equated with stupidity. Nor why on Earth a lack of feeling should be regarded as intelligent. Not yet at least. For it is The System's most insidious weapon against the sensitive and questioning mind. Only idiots feel. Smart people think.

"A nap? A *nap*?" I've got to *do* things! Summer is almost here and I don't even have a frigging bathroom! I need to act. Call someone to help me. Or...or...I don't know, I think I should at least panic a bit."

Grandmother Olive was silent. Her trunk was warm. I stared up into her boughs, into the myriad of pathways created by branches, each bifurcating to create new stems, and twigs. My eyes followed the woody roads as they cleaved themselves into greater and greater complexity. It was as though I was sitting under a gigantic ligneous nervous system. There was a clue here, I knew it. A clue to the secret of life. This branching from a stem, this relentless reaching out, the bifurcating pathways. It's a pattern you find all over nature, from brain stems, to plant structures, to blood vessels. It's something we all share. Humans. Animals. Trees. Plants. Something unequivocally Gaian.

Gaian. That was the last thing I remember, before the magic tree-smoke took me.

***

Half an hour later I awoke. Blinking, I put my hand out and touched Grandmother Olive's trunk. Slowly, I levered myself from the ground. But as I wandered back to the tent I knew something was different. I don't know how or why, but something or someone had pressed the reset button. It was as though a string of tech malware and old, data-sucking programs had been erased from my system.

Staring out over my land, I drank in the visuals. Everything was so clean and crisp, the colours so bright, I wondered vaguely if someone had spiked my water bottle while I wasn't looking. And then I remembered the tent shade.

In minutes I was standing over the wooden branches I'd collected from the forest earlier. They were jumbled on the dirt like broken femurs. Gaping into the small hole I'd dug in the soil, I pondered how to make it firmer, so that the post wouldn't wobble. Perhaps I could wedge something in there, something like...a rock.

Let time and light do the work.

Light and time. Of course, ideas take time to brew. But the light? What had Grandmother Olive meant by that?

The sun was now hurling heat at the land like a fast bowler, and working was going to be a slow, dogged fight against heatstroke. Standing up, I allowed my gaze to float over my slope. A few fat rocks poked their heads out of the ground, rocky scalps illuminated by the sun. They scintillated provocatively, which I took to be some sort of invitation. Gamely, I wandered down to dig the rocks out.

Once I'd collected a small heap of boulders, and had piled them up next to my tent, I stuck one of the branches in its pre-dug hole once more. Next, I rammed some of the largest rocks in around it. After that, I wedged smaller stones into the gaps so the larger ones couldn't move. Then I poured dry earth over the top and stamped down on it with my boot. Finally, the moment of truth. I gingerly pushed the branch with my hand. It stood fast. I pushed a bit harder. It stayed put. True, it wasn't going to withstand a heavy club swing, but it would do the job. I pulled the peak of my baseball cap down.

"Ha! You're stuck now, aren't you?" I gloated at the branch.

My new post was impervious to my glee. It simply stood there like a large, twisted sundial clocking up the minutes and hours. The sunlight slid steadily about its new axis. I continued to work. Three more branches and many gloats later I was feeling extremely pleased with myself. By now, the sun had arced behind my enchanted olive tree, and shadows had begun to bloom.

All that remained was to tie something over the top of my four posts to create a tent canopy of sorts. I'd drive to the town in the next few days and buy some shade cloth, but in the meantime a sarong would do. So I found a large purple one in one of my suitcases, and tied its four corners to the posts. That was that.

Buds of shade were now opening along the edges of the forest forming clumps of cool relief. The heat began to retreat. I felt my shoulders tingling from sunburn. Peering into my water canister, I decided there was just enough for a wash. So I carried the bottle to the edge of the forest and set it on a rock. Then I stared into the trees. The shadowy passageways beckoned me. They were curling wooden portals.

"Hey! Dirt Woman! I've made a shade. What do you say to that?" The forest said nothing. The air was still. The pine trees and wild carobs were unmoving. Even the crickets were quiet.

"I made it all by myself. A shade! Now the tent won't fry in the sun."

Still there was no reply. My words disappeared into darkness stretching between the humus and the canopy. I shrugged, and gave up. Reaching forward I touched the branch of one of the pines, and smiled. Home. This was home. The branch shivered as I released it, needles brushing against my fingers.

I turned to leave. And as I did, I caught the glint of white teeth.

The Invasion

"You're not lost up here, my dear. There's a guidebook you know."

It was only a couple of days later. I had already strung up a hammock up under Grandmother Olive, and was swinging in it, feeling the most peaceful person alive. The sun was inching from branch to branch leaving morning fast behind. The olive's leaves were pale green droplets and they hissed slightly in the breeze.

"A guidebook?" I murmured. Opening my eyes, I stared into the web of branches. Something beautiful filled me. I'd reached the outskirts of my mind's city and was on the fringes of somewhere new. Unpolluted. Instead of noisy tarmac highways, there were dirt lanes. Their verges were grassy and winked with forget-me-nots, daisies, and vetch.

"Well, if there *is* a guidebook, tell me about it. I feel clueless to be honest. Where is it? Have you got it?"

Grandmother Olive shook as a breeze began to play with the green bouquets she held in her spiny hands. It looked as though she were chortling, and I felt a prickle creep up my back.

"Nature is the book!" My tree spoke loudly now, the words reverberating within me like a gong. "You dipped into its muddy pages when you created your *wonderful* wash rack."

Brightening at the thought of my wash rack, I sat up a little. The hammock ropes were tight on my flesh, and I could feel parts of my rump falling through the holes. A thought inched across my mind, slowly, like a buried animal waking from hibernation. I started to see what Grandmother Olive meant.

"Ah yes, I looked at the valley, and that's where I got the idea of how to make the rack."

At that moment, a large agama lizard, a male, poked his crusty old head around the side of the tree trunk, black bead-eyes darting up, down, and back. He stuck effortlessly onto his knotty vertical perch, apparently defying gravity. I gaped a little as the agama's craggy crown nodded up and down. A flurry of emotions whipped about in my chest. The lizard felt so close. So amazingly similar to me.

Swinging both legs out of the hammock, I pulled myself into a sitting position. The sun was now directly overhead. The crickets were chanting. They sounded like the devotees of some odd, six-legged cult. I tilted my head back once more, staring into the thick boughs. Finally, I realised the obvious. The thoughts and words were mine, but the *tree* somehow kindled them within me. Just as the land had inspired the dirt woman, the olive tree was opening my brain up to another kind of wisdom. And it wasn't an 'it' at all. The tree was a living being with her own will to live, and her own aura. A chemical reaction was taking place between me and her, and she was changing me.

Years later I learned that I wasn't in fact the crazy, over-imaginative noodle I thought I was. Seven years in the future, I would listen to a podcast by the world-renowned biochemist Diana Beresford-Kroeger. She would explain how the Earth's forests act as aerosols for various beneficial biochemical compounds, and that these chemicals penetrate our cell membranes, provoking any number of transformations. One of these arboreal aroma compounds is beta-ionone which has the ability to switch off rogue genes in the DNA and to turn off prostate cancer cells, among other things[2].

I hadn't known the science back then though. All I knew was my experience. Since I had arrived here in this land, I had felt different. Thought differently. Behaved differently. The terrain of my reality was starting to

---

2   . There are many academic articles on the effect of plant and tree aroma on human health. Ethyl Acetate, for example, has been found to cause cytotoxicity in breast cancer cells (without even coming in contact with the culture medium and cells). **"Effect of ethyl acetate aroma on viability of human breast cancer and normal kidney epithelial cells *in vitro,*"** Mohsin A. Khan, Rumana Ahmad, Anand N. Srivastava. Published *Integrative Medicine Research*, Volume 6, Issue 1, p47-59

morph into something, well...psychedelic. And this isn't so strange really. When I consider the amount of mind-altering plants in the world; peyote, poppy, ayahuasca, psilocybin, cannabis, and salvia to name but a few, it stands to reason that all plants have some sort of effect upon us. And that we don't necessarily have to ingest them. Inhaling their aroma must also influence us in some some way.

"Look for clues in the soil, the animals, and the trees, especially the trees. They are all moving from the same essence," Grandmother Olive whispered. "They are connected to the whole story, rather than perceiving fragmented pieces of it like modern humans do."

Lying back in the hammock, I let it swing gently. The rope creaked as it moved. Air murmured through the parasol of leaves and brushed across my cheeks. The sky filled in the gaps between the branches. It was a completed jigsaw of the purest azure. And I sensed how much more I was than this body in this hammock. How much richer I was than the dry skeleton of my thoughts. I felt the movement between inside and outside. The exchange of chemicals, and who knew what else?

And then, just as I was sinking into this wonderland, without the slightest warning, someone uninvited broke in.

"Naber? How's it going there?"

Shocked out of my trance, I leaped from the hammock. Who the hell was it? Who was here?

There, striding up my slope, I saw a grey-haired fellow with a baseball cap perched on his head. As he drew nearer, I could see he touted a large moustache and ravenous eyes. He was all over me even from twenty metres.

I knew who it was. The chap who owned the greenhouses below. He didn't live here, but sometimes came to work in his polytunnels. Despite this, I felt invaded. This was my space. My private sanctuary. Not a common thoroughfare.

"Came to say hello, to see what's up. I'm Talip." He was still striding.

Now, I don't think I'm being unfair when I say that boundaries, if they exist at all, are a blurry affair in Turkey. No one has a concept of personal space, privacy, or borders. Even the word 'private' doesn't really exist in its own right. '*Ozel*' means both special and private, and the distinction is never particularly clear. Romantic (and lonely) Westerners who haven't spent a couple of decades in communal societies tend to think this is all just wonderful, because individualism is their curse. Let me tell you, there are other curses.

"So you're the new neighbour, eh? Living in a tent? Alone?" Talip reached my terrace. It didn't escape me how fast he'd climbed the sharp incline, and how he wasn't out of breath. The maturing man clutched a small pick in one hand, and a cigarette in the other. He stood there for a minute, sucking on his *sigara*, eyeing me up and down as though I was his favourite meal.

Now having lived in Turkey a long time, I knew the ropes. Never be too nice. Never look scared. Always move from a position of power, whichever form you possess (and a good sixty per cent of power is psychological). I stiffly advanced on the man and pulled on the classroom-management personality from my years of teaching secondary-school boys in the UK.

"Hello, Talip. How can I help you?"

My stance and my coolness smacked into his voracity. He slowed his advance.

"Just saying hello, like. I always walk through here to get to the other side."

"Well, I'm here now, Talip, and I've come for peace and quiet. But hello." I held out my hand for a formal greeting. Talip ventured forward and gripped my palm. His eyes were rolling and squirming all over the place like a pair of ocular eels.

Then all of a sudden the eels stopped wriggling. Something else had caught Talip's attention. He had spied a stubborn thistle protruding to his left. To my horror, this intruder raised his pick, and in one deft swing destroyed the plant.

I gaped at the dead scrag of thorns now strewn in the dirt. I was incensed. The outrage surged into every muscle. And it was then she bolted out of the forest, teeth gnashing, saliva dripping from her mouth, eye-whites showing. Dirt Woman pounded over to the fat thistle Talip had killed, and knelt next to it. She stared at it for one long second, before standing and turning on the farmer. She wanted to kill him. I wanted to kill him. We were completely on the same page.

In one way of course Talip didn't see the bared incisors. But in another way he did. He shifted his feet a little and fiddled with the pick handle.

"Need to get rid of those things. They grow as big as trees and then you'll never cut them out."

I made strong eye contact, and moved forward. Abruptly, I felt the Dirt Woman in my flesh, in my bones, staring out through my eyes. It was quite a sensation. Her power was pure and vital. "Never do that again please. This is my land. Killing is not allowed. Neither is smoking. This is a special space. It's *sacred*."

The words came from somewhere else. Until that moment I hadn't really voiced it. Rules seemed so authoritarian, so dictatorial. But suddenly, in the face of this intrusion, I didn't care. I was sick of conforming to etiquette, and of acquiescing to the insensitive and brutish.

Dirt Woman paced between Talip and I, growling quietly.

Talip blanched. Then his cheeks flushed pink. Disgusted, he threw his cigarette into the dust and stamped on it. I knew only too well just how rude I had been. In Turkey a guest can do whatever they like, because according to Islam they are from God. Oh and don't these guests just know it? I've seen the hospitality cow milked so dry the poor beast collapses in the dust.

I stepped toward the disgruntled farmer, and lowered my voice a little.

"It's not personal, Talip. I'm going to say the same to everyone. The land spoke to me. I have to listen to it."

Now, in a Western country where mysticism and magic were long ago slaughtered by the machete of 'reason', this comment would probably have been met by contempt, especially from a man like Talip. But one of the benefits of living in Turkey was that the locals still held a reverence for myth and spirit. Nearly all of them, male and female, possessed an excellent understanding of intuition and energy. I'll be honest, they *had* to to survive. There wasn't much of a system in rural Anatolia, nothing functioned as it 'should', disaster could strike at any given time and there really wasn't much you could do about it. Planning counted for nothing at all. The government changed laws at the drop of a hat. And if you reached the end of the year without a coup, financial collapse, or an earthquake, you felt you'd done well. There was only one way to navigate such unpredictable waters – intuition. And there was a common understanding among village folk, that women knew more about this than men. If you wanted your coffee cup read or your dreams analysed, it was a *teze* (auntie) you deferred to. I owe many things to my years in Turkey, but if I had any ability at all to hear my land and feel its power in the beginning, it's down to the underground rural shamanism of Anatolia.

Talip stared at the dust for a moment. His features were still tight, but his pride had been rescued. He didn't laugh at me. He didn't even question it. The land had spoken. I had heard it. He nodded, albeit curtly.

"Would you like a drink of water?" I said.

"Yeah. Bit hot walking up here."

I fetched a glass and filled it. An understanding had been reached.

***

Ten minutes later I watched the white of Talip's shirt disappear through the sprawl of Mediterranean oaks at the bottom of my land. The afternoon was loosening, the heat edging back into the sky a little. Sighing, I wandered wandered in the direction of Grandmother Olive. A sadness began to pluck away somewhere under my collar bone. Why did it always have to be this way? Why do you always have to fight?

"You do good thing."

I paused and turned. Dirt Woman was hovering about ten metres from me. She fixed her deep black eyes on mine. They were tunnels stretching back to another planet Earth, one I was becoming more and more curious about, one that was perhaps still concealed within this one.

"I think *you* did it, didn't you?"

Dirt Woman shook her head. "You do it. When you real and no be afraid of your culchure, you have power. Because real is real. And lie is lie. Lie never win. Pretend never win. He know you real. He know you right."

"He was angry, didn't you see? It may cause me trouble later." I felt my lungs deflate.

The dirt woman opened her wide brown mouth and guffawed. It was a loud and raucous laugh that echoed from the hillside. "He no make trouble now. He understand. You are real, land is ours, and I am here."

I cocked my head to one side and took her in, the purity of her gaze, the shine of her skin. For the first time, I started to see just how beautiful she was. How – as she quite rightly put it – real. Dirt Woman remained there, gleaming in the sunlight, while I moved under the canopy of the olive tree and pulled the hammock toward me. It was then I remembered something.

Turning around, I asked, "Do you hear the trees speak?"

The dirt woman looked at Grandmother Olive. Then she gazed at the other two large olives, one curvaceous tree below, and one scrawnier above. She bowed her head a little. "I hear all tree. And animal. And flower. And rock. Everything talk and listen. But not with word. We don't need word. That's why I no speak good. Words so...so...I no like! They cut world into small square, and give all wrong idea."

The olive leaves crackled a little as a late-afternoon breath of wind pushed through them.

"But this tree seems to be speaking so fluently, using lots of words, amazing words." I sat down in the hammock and lifted my feet off the ground. My lips pulled together over my teeth as I concentrated.

Slowly, Dirt Woman approached the tree. And again her features drew apart. She looked wary. Dropping to a squat under the three fat columns of the olive's trunk, she pressed her lips to the bark. Eyes closed, head resting on the trunk, Dirt Woman began to speak.

"This tree is a special one," she said. "She is the great-grandmother, and she talks to all the other trees and plants on the land, in *all* their languages. She is a translator."

My head snapped round, because all of a sudden Dirt Woman was speaking in perfectly conjugated English. My ancient landmate abruptly pulled back from the tree. Her chest heaved as she gulped in air. She looked winded. Slowly she crawled out of the shade, and collapsed back into the sun. I sprang out of the hammock and followed her.

"What in hell just happened?" I asked.

"So much idea. So much idea. If I say all idea coming from Great-Grandmother Tree now, you go crazy. If you know all forest secret, may be you run away. And you no must run away. You must stay."

Quickly she pulled herself to her feet. Then she did something quite out of character. She reached forward and stroked my hair.

"Why must I stay?"

Dirt Woman stared at me. There was a desperation in her eyes. One I'd never seen or noticed before.

"Because if you go, I die!" she said, tears welling up in her eyes. Then she turned, and galloped into the arms of the forest.

Garden Angel

The water glugged happily into a ten-litre plastic bottle. I marvelled at the tap, the simple turning of it and the subsequent cord of water that poured out. What convenience! What luxury to be able to just twist a piece of metal and be provided with endless H2O.

It wasn't my tap. It was Dudu's. I was replenishing my stock. Three or four chickens squawked about the spigot, orange feathers ruffling. We were shaded by an enormous grape vine. The large leaves hid clusters of baby grapes. It was only May, and they'd take a couple of months to swell into sweet Dionysus fruit.

Dudu opened her ramshackle gate. It was no more than a few thin planks and corrugated plastic all nailed haphazardly together. "Look, here he is!" she cried as she dragged the misshapen assemblage noisily over the ground. A tiny walnut of a man skipped round the corner of her house. He squinted shyly in the mid-afternoon sun, his face all wrinkles and moustache.

"This is Celal. I told you about him, remember. He's the fella you need to get rid of that grass!" Dudu squawked.

A large dog sidled up to us, and barged past Celal. It was an Anatolian shepherd, as striking in its hugeness as Celal was in his smallness. It had a black face, a long pink tongue, and looked like a cross between a wolf and a lion. I took a step back. The hound rushed toward me panting heavily.

"Oh my God! Is he safe?"

"Oh, Apo's alright." Dudu stepped past the dog, and it loped off, tongue lolling, to the chickens' water bowl.

"Don't you be a-worryin'. Apo's as good as gold," said Celal, even more wrinkles congregating about his eyes. He was wearing a dilapidated pair of jeans, a checked shirt, and a pair of derelict court shoes with the backs crushed down. The shoes were no doubt as old as my car.

"This is the English woman I told you about, living in the tent over there," said Dudu.

"Aye," said Celal and stretched out a hand eagerly. "The crazy one." He chortled to himself as if it were the most hilarious joke in the world. "Pleased to meet yer and welcome to our neighbour'ood."

"Pleased to meet you too, Celal," I said. I shook the hand firmly, noting how strong it was considering how small a body it was attached to.

Dudu hitched up her şalwars and pushed Celal to one side. It didn't escape me that he kept being shoved out of the way, either by his dog or his neighbour. Shifting between us, she placed a confiding hand on my upper arm. "Celal helps the English, the *other* English, down the road," she said. "He's a good sort, ever so trustworthy. The other English leave their key with him and everything. He normally works for fifty lira a day, but because we know each other..." she winked, "and because you're a neighbour and a bit poor by the looks of things, he'll work for forty lira for you."

I frowned. I wasn't sure I wanted anyone to help me. Over the years, I'd had plenty of experience of workmen hacking down favourite bushes, talking too much and generally generating more mess than they resolved. Turning in the direction of my land, I peered over the green spikiness of the pomegranate trees, straining to see my tent. It was invisible from Dudu's house, which I was happy about.

"So when can I start?" Celal said brightly. "I'm good at grass cuttin'. I can take care of yer plot in a day."

"A day? You can cut all that grass in a *day*?" I blinked in disbelief. It had taken me a day to clear a piece the size of a Turkish carpet. That the skinny little gremlin before me would be capable of such shearing was inconceivable.

"Snot much there, juss grass innit?" Celal shrugged.

I weighed it up. Forty lira for the entire field of grass cut. It was an attractive offer. I'd probably earn it from my first yoga class. And it would free me up to get on with the mountain of other jobs on my to-do list.

"Alright then," I said, turning to Celal and straightening. "Forty bucks it is. Are you free tomorrow?"

"Aye." Celal grinned. "I'll be there at eight o'clock. And I'll bring a scythe. You need a good scythe for that lot."

I held out my hand to shake on the deal. Celal squeezed my palm between two rough brown hands. Dudu folded her arms over her chest and pushed her chin forward. She looked exceedingly pleased with herself.

***

I awoke, as usual, with the light and the birds. The valley was still a dark corridor, but the sky blazed pink and orange. I only had a couple of hours before Celal would arrive. A stab of anxiety flashed into my throat when I remembered that. This beautiful land, it was so precious. Damn! Why did I hire him? What was I thinking? He'd murder everything. They always did. The more I thought about it the crosser I became, so I stopped pondering and pulled myself out of bed.

I'd now been on the land for no more than a couple of weeks. Yet it was as though invisible earth tentacles had wound themselves around me. I had become so attached to the place. Like a mother to a child, or was it a child to a mother? Yes, who was protecting who here?

Yawning, I crawled from my tent, reaching for a comb on my way out. Then I stretched and faced the valley. The view was divine. Thousands upon thousands of deep green pines swept to the valley floor. The sun had just hit their crowns and they sparkled, acre upon acre of them, under its touch. As I brushed the tangles and dirt out of my hair, I felt the freest person alive.

After inhaling a few deep breaths, I wandered out of the land and over to the forest at the rear which had become my poop spot. As I squatted I made note: the next job was to build a toilet, a composting one like I'd seen on an eco-farm near Isparta. It had looked fairly straightforward. I'd need some plywood and nails, and a hammer, though.

***

"Morning there, neighbour! *Afiyet olsun.*"

Craning my head back I saw my new garden help staring over at me from Dudu's side of the fence. He had a red baseball cap on and a scythe, pick, and rake resting on his shoulder.

"You brought tools? You didn't need to. I have those," I said between chomps of fried egg.

"Aye, but you never know if they're any good. I trust nowt but me own tools." Celal was still staring at me. I was sitting in front of my tent with a glass of tea in my hand and must have looked...well, interesting. Finally, Celal stopped gawping and wandered around the fence to the entrance on the eastern side of the land. It was then I saw Apo the dog close on his heel. This golden fur-beast trotted down the path, his long tail curled up over his backside. He sniffed a little, then cocked a leg on one of the dog roses, before cantering in my direction. I eyed him dubiously. His head was twice the size of mine.

"Are you sure Apo is safe?" I said. "I mean, do you think he'd turn nasty if pushed the wrong way?"

"Only if you're a male dog, and then he's a right pain in the arse, fighting and the like. But people? Nah. Told yer, he's good as gold."

Apo brushed against my thigh and then stuck his muzzle in my groin. I stood there and flinched. Irritation flowered inside me. The dog. The scythe. It was too early and I didn't want to see anyone. Not here. And definitely not this undersized munchkin man who was going to cut everything and kill it. Why oh *why* had I hired him? The traffic in my head surged pell-mell into a tunnel. A bottleneck was beginning, and I could see hazard lights flashing in front and behind.

Celal adjusted his cap and looked left and right. "Where d'you want me to start?"

Fighting my way out of my mental congestion, I straightened my shoulders. Then I scanned my land. "Erm. Why don't you begin over here by the olives and then work across the top. The most important part is this plateau."

Celal dropped his tools under the olive tree, retaining only the scythe. Then he hunched over, grabbed a handful of grass, and began slicing through the stalks. I turned back to my breakfast plate, but was scrutinising the scene out of the corner of my eye. Both the land and the air were still. The sound of the scythe splitting the grass was as rhythmic as the throb of the crickets. Every muscle in my body tensed as I obsessively followed Celal's progress.

After a few minutes, he spoke. "I'm guessing you want me to leave these green plants 'ere."

Swivelling round from the washing-up rack, I gawked at him. He was clutching a soft leaved bush in his hand. I'd never even noticed it until that moment because it had been consumed by the grass.

"Oh. Yes. That's right. My God! I thought you'd just wipe the whole lot out."

"Nah. The rule is if iss got spikes it goes, if iss green it stays, at least in my book."

I nodded slowly and wondrously. "Oh, there's something else I forgot to say. There's no killing on my land. No killing of animals."

"Everything's got a right to live. I agree with yer there. Once killed a snake I did. Long and black it was. And it gave me such a bad look when I killed it. I'll never forget that look. Like it was cursin' me or something. After that I swore I'd never kill one of 'em again."

I put down the washing-up sponge and stared at Celal slack-jawed. Never in all my time of living around these parts, had I heard a local say anything like that. I looked over at Apo. He was flopped under the olive tree snoozing. Then I looked back at Celal. He'd lovingly cleared the grass from around the bush now, and it sprung up, green and lush.

"Stay green all summer this one will. Funny plant, never dries out. Smells a bit off, but looks okay, dunnit?"

"Beautiful!" I applauded.

We both admired it for a moment, and then Celal bent over again and continued cutting. Folding my arms across my chest, I spent a good few minutes mooning over that shrub, before turning to study the small hunched shape of Celal. His oversized jeans barely held onto his hips. But his arms were strong. One weathered hand held the grass stalks, while the other deftly sliced them away. The dry grass fell, green leaves appeared, and the thorn bushes became a large, barbed heap.

As the sun crawled over its apex, I strode toward Grandmother Olive. She was cool and peaceful, as always. Lifting my legs into the hammock, I watched Celal from my rope cradle, but restlessness pushed and pulled at my psyche. How difficult it was for me to relax, because I felt I should be doing something. Anything. There was so much to do after all.

I swung. The tree stirred. Her small green leaves turned gently in the breeze as her arboreal soul began to murmur. Soon enough an idea dropped from her boughs, directly into my head.

"Celal? Are you free in a couple of days to work again?" I called over the land.

Celal stood up a moment and squinted in my direction. "Aye."

"Good! I need to make a place to teach yoga down in the valley. We'll make it together."

***

Yes, we could create the space. But that didn't mean it would work. It didn't mean anything at all.

Two days later Celal drove down to the valley to Café Cactus. What a happy afternoon the pair of us spent, digging and rock-shifting, raking and soil-flattening. I loved the sensation of the earth under my hands, the cool peaty smell, the clicking and knocking of the rocks. By evening a gorgeous terrace had been cleared amidst the orange trees. It was perfect.

Two more days after that, I was standing on my new yoga terrace in a pair of violet Aladdin pants. I dug my bare toes into the soft kilims I'd just bought. A Dutch couple towered in front of me in blond magnificence. Their arms were stretched over their heads and their legs were bent in the warrior pose. I watched as they inhaled and exhaled, eyes closed in concentration.

But something was wrong. Not with the yogis. Not with the space. With *me*. I felt as though an invisible hand was grabbing my throat and throttling me.

Breathing deeply, I hoped the sensation would go away. But it didn't. With each new pose, I lost more and more patience. The orange trees rustled slightly, their leaves waving like dark green fingers. I had one leg bent in the tree pose. My body was a machine, a well-oiled robot following the commands of its driver. But my skin was crawling. Nausea. Boredom. They were all over me. It didn't escape me that I'd enjoyed clearing the space for the class more than I was enjoying teaching it.

I closed my eyes, opened them again. And then I saw her sinewy body winding its way through the orange trees, half-lynx, half-ape. Her eyes were caves, and in the backs of them I saw fires burning.

"Why you no be real?" Leaning forward, Dirt Woman kissed my cheek before stepping past me. I smelt the musk of organic, unprocessed sweat, and something inside me ached. How I thirsted to follow her! Because despite the fact that she was destroying my economic prospects, she *was* real. Uncompromisingly. Unashamedly. And I knew she held the fronds of something I'd lost long ago. Life. Earthy, full-blooded life.

As the yoga session dragged on, I scratched at my arms, trying to peel off the choreographed niceties of the 'civilised' world. The empty smiles. The staged caring. The stifled yawns. It was all a charade. The whole damn thing. What was I doing here 'teaching' when I had nothing of any value to teach?

The Dutch couple were laying prostrate on their kilims, legs splayed and eyes closed in the corpse pose. Finally, we were reaching the end of what was for me the most arduous yoga session of my life. I took them through the guided relaxation.

"Reeelaaax. Reeelaaax," I intoned into the sweet-smelling air of the orange grove.

But inside, a voice was screaming. And it wasn't saying *relax*. Because if I had to say that word one more time, I'd murder someone. Gaskets began blowing. Steam billowed from cracks in the pipes. Systems crashed. Pistons squealed. And finally the engine of bullshit ground to a halt.

Once the couple had left, I began folding up the kilims. And I knew. I couldn't teach another lesson. *Ever*. It was over. When I realised this, I felt sick all the way to my duodenum. I'd always been a teacher. I had nothing else to fall back on. How on Earth was I going to get by?

The Land Guardian

The sun was setting. Even though my eyes were closed, I could sense the light turning from amber to violet. The nutty smell of my bamboo mat drifted into my nose. Snapping my eyes open, I found myself staring into an enigma of a sky. Twilight was swimming in our direction in swift cloudless strokes, as always brandishing his magic casket of power. But I didn't care. I had no intention of using it. It was twenty-four hours after my final yoga debacle, and I was still brooding.

I hugged my knees to my chest. A heavy pout settled into my mouth and chin. All was lost now. The city of my mind seemed to have suffered a black-out, the busy offices of my hopes and plans were now engulfed in darkness. Fear had long left the train station of my emotions. Another engine had pulled into the platform: despair. As the shrouded passengers poured out of their carriages and trudged wearily through the turnstiles, I bit my lip.

Dusk flooded my land. It gushed over the slope and into the nooks and crannies, a gossamer veil of mystery. The trees twisted. The leaves shrank. As I stared into the deepening gloom, the rocks began to glimmer. They protruded like knuckles on a hand that was gripping something very tightly. What? What was my land holding onto with such veracity?

"How am I going to survive?" I bleated to the land. My words rolled down the slope, verbal tears on a dirt face.

But twilight doesn't simply hold power pockets. It hides other secrets. Other magic. Because when the sun bows below the skyline, and darkness comes out to play, so do the earth spirits and the land guardians. The voices within the trees, rocks, and hills, all become audible.

"Why you cry? Survive is very easy!" It was Dirt Woman's voice, and it came from a pine tree in her forest. I saw the needles of the tree flutter, the branches bend, before a brown body slid onto the ground.

"I've always been a teacher! I thought it was the reason I was here," I muttered.

My dirt friend scampered over to me. She eschewed my bamboo mat and squatted in the dust in front of me. "You here because you here. Why you need reason?"

But her words didn't console me. I'd lost my purpose, and this terrible truth made me feel quite light-headed. "I don't know, but I do. I can't just *exist*!"

For the millionth time, Dirt Woman gawped at me nonplussed. She stuck her generous lips out and rolled her eyes. "Me no understand. To be modern woman is very...very bad. Oof so difficult!"

I nodded. That my sense of self had been so tightly tethered to something as ephemeral as a job was indeed distressing. I buried my head in my knees and mumbled. "Do you think I can survive without a job?"

"You *human*! You have much power. Why you think you need this job thing?" Dirt Woman then broke wind both loudly and proudly, which didn't help my mood.

Jerking my head up, I pulled the edges of my face into a scowl. "Because unlike you I can't live without money, or a bit of civilisation," I grumbled.

"You are dirt child. Listen dirt and listen tree. Learn listening very good then you never be hungry. All land and forest work to-ge-ther. They hide many secret, and you must listen so you hear them."

"I...I just don't think I'm up to it."

Dirt Woman reached over and slapped me square on the shoulder. Then she stood up and scanned the sky. Her tight flesh relaxed, and her face grew still and calm. Both her bare feet were planted firmly in the soil, and her hair, knotted as it was, stirred in the darkening air. I just knew she was connecting to something. Something I still didn't comprehend or completely trust.

"Land even show you money paper secret when you ready," my dirt friend said somewhat mysteriously. Then she exhaled, eyes clicking back into focus. And without further ado, she trotted back to the pines, leaving me to my grump.

A warm wind rushed up the slope. All the trees in the forest began to rustle and sway excitedly. I turned my head in the direction of Grandmother Olive and saw she was glowing faintly. Remembering her effect on me, and her ability to provoke another kind of thinking, I stood up and walked over to her. The thick plumes of foliage created an inky world where twilight had been and gone. I rested my back against Grandmother Olive's trunk feeling knots of bark rubbing against my vertebrae. Then I closed my eyes. The leaves rustled ever so gently. Peace began to descend.

"You know this is a *special* piece of land, don't you?" The words tumbled into me.

"What do you mean?" I asked, eyes still closed.

"It's protected by a spirit. It's protecting *you*. You are quite safe, my dear."

Opening my eyes a little, I raised my brows doubtfully. "How do you know?"

"I can see him."

"The spirit? Where?" I sat up and began to strain my eyes. This was all turning a little too flaky for my liking. "What do you mean by a spirit?"

"What do you mean by it?" Came the tree's retort. And it made me consider what we mean when we talk of anything non-physical. The English language may comprise a wealth of words for describing external objects, but for the internal world? Compared to Turkish, it's an impoverished wasteland. Turkish has words for emotions that monolingual Anglo-Saxons don't even *feel*[3]. It has at least four words for soul, and many for subtle energies and spirits. There was no inquisition in Turkish history, no witch burning, nor much persecution of seers and mystics, in the way there was in Europe. As a result the language pertaining to all things of the spirit has

---

[3]   One example of this would be the Turkish word "hüzün". It's an emotion that is neither positive nor negative, and denotes a type of melancholic sadness that is incredibly beautiful and almost delectable. I only really grasped this emotion after speaking Turkish for about 10 years, and the experience made me consider much about how group consciousness affects the mind.

remained relatively pure, whereas English words concerning anything magical have been manipulated deformed over the past five hundred years to such an extent, even to mention magic gives many folk the As it goes for witches, so it goes for spirits.

"He's over there on the ridge. And he can take on different forms too, like a shape-shifter," my mind was humming now with the ideas the tree provoked.

I spun about, searching the land. The air had now turned the colour of smoke, and I peered into the grey, trying to spot something. I saw nothing.

"No no, you don't see spirits like that!" Grandmother Olive swished her outer branches. She was a green sorceress waving her arms.

"How do you see them then?"

"In your imagination."

I snorted and flopped back against the olive's trunk. "Oh well, that's convenient, isn't it? So basically I can imagine whatever I like, and according to you, it's a spirit. I could imagine the world is riding on the back of a giant turtle, or that the universe was created by a teapot."

"But you didn't see a teapot, did you?" Again that strange warm wind blew, and the leaves whooshed soothingly. Later on, once I'd become more adept at Earth-whispering, the wind and shaking foliage would become a sign to me, a sign that some sort of communication was happening. That I was hitting the correct 'thought note' so to speak. But not yet. All I knew was that my skin prickled.

"I didn't see an image at all," I said, more quietly now.

"Oh my dear, you mustn't imagine *randomly*. Everything is interconnected – me, you, the land and the spirits. All spirits are really just parts of the mind, but the trouble is you've been taught that the mind is in your head. How can it be, when it's not a physical reality at all? It's another realm."

I nodded. That was already clear to me. Having already completed two vipassana meditations where I sat for ten days at a time without speaking, I'd learned a thing or two about that. I remembered one experience where I literally shifted from a state of being in acute physical pain (which tends to happen when you sit cross-legged for ten hours a day) to a place where pain didn't exist any more. In one reality the pain was there. In another it wasn't. While the brain may be the physical radio receiver, the mind is something else.

"So if it's not just about thinking any old random thing, what does it mean to see a spirit then?"

"You must allow images to bloom in *response* to the land. Open your senses and let your surroundings speak to you. Let the dirt inspire you."

I stared into the dusk. The slope was now a pale strip of stubble with the forested darkness closing in at the edges. Inhaling, I smelt dry grass and pine sap. My nose twitched. I could smell bark too. And wet earth where I'd poured the contents of my washing-up bowl. An exotic cult of crickets was trilling behind me, while a couple of late birds chirped their goodnights. Every now again there was a light whoosh as the breeze moved leaves.

I screwed up my forehead, and pondered. Then I stopped pondering and started feeling. It was true. I *did* feel protected. Safe. I always had up here, from the very first night. If I hadn't felt that, I'd have never have moved up here in the first place. And under this olive tree was the place I felt most safe of all, unassailable even.

"Now let the land guardian appear to you. Or speak to you." The tree was whispering so quietly now, I had no idea whether her words were thoughts or the breeze.

The grey deepened to the colour of lead. Night began to waft in. And then I saw him in my mind's eye. He was a druid-like fellow. White. With a crook. Though what a druid was doing in southern Turkey was anyone's guess. He didn't say anything. He just stood there. But he was very old. Ancient. But almost as soon as I caught sight of him, he disappeared, back into the recesses of my subconscious.

Opening my eyes, I stared about, half-expecting to see the guardian on the brow of the hill. Slowly I clambered out of the hammock and wandered over to the entrance of my land. I was still thinking.

When I stood at the mouth of my plot – the exact spot where it joined the forest – I shuddered. What it was, I couldn't put my finger on. It was as though there was a magic ring encircling my land, and the moment I stepped beyond it, particularly on the northern edge where the fearsome forest stood, a distinct chill would slither up my torso. Yet when I stepped back, I was safe. Home. And the chill turned to warmth.

Was there really a land guardian here? Or was I feeling what I wanted to feel? Or was there another truth, and that what I felt was in some way reflecting back to me? Perhaps it was none of these things. Perhaps all of them combined.

The slope was now steeped in dusk, the outlines of the forest blurring. I was breathing enchantment, so I decided to experiment.

Slowly I stepped up the path, beyond the border of my land. I trod gingerly toward the fearsome forest to see how far I could go before I felt unprotected. I didn't take more than a couple of steps. Such a terror grabbed me, I couldn't lift a foot.

I stood and gaped up at the enormous pines at the forest edge. They patrolled the front lines of the battle between forest and man. Even in the darkness, I saw their thick trunks. They were leviathans stretching higher than a small apartment block. Their canopies were huge fists of needles. Staring at them awestruck, I felt an absurd desire to drop to my knees. The pines held their positions.

My skin grew spikes. I gulped, forcing myself to remain put. To feel it. I managed about half a minute, before I turned and ran. There was no getting away from it. Out there by the forest, I felt I was open to every horror the wild could throw at me. And I couldn't put my finger on why. There were but a few metres of earth between my plot and those trees. What difference could a few metres make?

Skidding down the path, I galloped into my land. As soon as I breached the border, the atmosphere changed. It was palpable. I was safe again.

I belted for all I was worth to my tent. Still shuddering, I opened the hatch and threw myself inside. I yanked off my boots, and left them upturned on my bamboo mat balcony. Then I zipped up the door, checking the opening with my fingers to make sure nothing could enter. Finally, I sprawled onto my sleeping bag fully clothed and stared out at the lights of Alakır. They formed a distant crescent. Night was here.

I gurgled and shook. I tried to find my fear. I wanted to trap it and stuff it in a jam jar, to observe it safely. But it was running about my body, all hackles and cold flushes. I couldn't seem to get near it. Perhaps I didn't need to. Because that self-same fear was about to get very near *me*. Just as I closed my eyes, I heard a heavy rustle.

The noise was coming from behind my tent! I felt every muscle flex. My ears stretched out from the sides of my head like radio dishes. That was when I heard the padding of feet. Large animal feet. Jerking my eyelids apart, I gulped at the darkness pouring in. There was no light. Nothing to see.

Another scuffle. Something was sniffing the edge of my tent! And whatever it was, it wasn't small. My heart lurched. The panic button in my mind was pressed. Boar. *Boar*! Oh shit! It had to be a boar, nothing else was that big. An image of a tusk ripping through my canvas-bubble rose up. My heart cranked up once again. It pumped so hard and fast my ears throbbed.

I heard grass being flattened. And an intense panting. But...that panting...there was something familiar about it. Finally, it occurred to me. Perhaps it wasn't a boar after all, because there *was* another animal in the vicinity large enough to make this sort of noise.

Grabbing my torch, I slid over to the hatch. Carefully, I unzipped it. Holding my breath, I poked my head gingerly out of my tent. And who should be slumped next to me, tongue lolling and grinning, but Apo the dog.

Never have I been so glad to see a hound. Apo stood up, all wet nose and saliva, nearly as tall as my tent. I stretched my hand out and stroked between his ears. His fur was as thick as a bear's. Raising his massive head, he proudly surveyed the slope before emitting three or four impressively loud barks. They rebounded all the way down the slope and rolled along the road far below.

Apo was an Anatolian shepherd and he was genetically wired to protect. Nothing, neither human nor animal, was going to enter this land with him around. Why Apo had taken it upon himself to guard me, I had no idea. But I wasn't the first or the last to remark there was something very mythical about Apo the dog. Something wise and soulful.

Closing the hatch again, I smiled. Then I slumped back onto my sleeping bag, and shut my eyes feeling as safe as a babe in a crib. I heard Apo outside emit a contented sigh. And it felt good. So very good to have a land guardian. And just like that I stopped worrying about survival and jobs and earning money. Because I could see there were other powers at work. Powers I wanted to know more about.

Shit Box

As the sun climbed over the pine tops, I happily munched on a feast of filter coffee, eggs, tomatoes, and olives. And while I digested my food, the workforce of my mind punched in. Sitting down at their desks, it didn't take long for the suits to start printing out action plans and to-do lists. Time was of the essence. I had only a month left before summer stamped us all into human-shaped dollops of pizza dough.

I didn't know it as I swigged my coffee, but this was also going to be the first day I used a hammer. It was probably the poorest effort at nail-banging the world of woodwork has ever seen, but we all have to start somewhere, don't we?

"Mornin', neighbour. And how's it going today then?" Celal's sun-crinkled face peered down at me from Dudu's land. I'd decided to get him to come once every two weeks for the next couple of months, just to get me started. Today was one of his days. I raised the thumb on my right hand at him and grinned, before pouring him a mug of coffee. His red baseball cap disappeared behind the woman-eating thorn bushes at the back of the land, before reappearing at the entrance. Apo wasn't trotting behind him today, because he was sitting next to me, tongue hanging out.

"Ah, I wondered where he'd got to," Celal nodded at his dog as he walked toward the olive tree where I was sitting. "Don't feed him. Or he'll never come home."

"Alright, I promise I won't. I did give him some bread this morning, because he watched over me all night." I gazed at Apo lovingly. He sat like the sphinx, paws stretched in front of him, basking in my praise. "He's stayed here a few nights now."

"Aye, he likes yer."

Celal bopped on a stool and heaped spoon after spoon of sugar into his coffee. He didn't say any more about Apo's new moonlighting number, but I couldn't help but notice the puff of irritation lingering in the air.

"So what we up to today then?" Celal sipped at his mug and smacked his lips.

"A toilet," I announced. "A composting toilet."

Celal's already wrinkle-ridden brow became a forest of haphazard lines. He shifted on his stool and swilled his coffee about his mug.

"Basically, it's a wooden box," I said, pushing my own mug away from me.

"A box," Celal repeated. "So where's your shit gonna go? We gonna dig a hole for it?"

"Nope. It sits in the box. A friend of mine did it in Isparta. I think I've got the idea, so we can copy it."

Celal squinted at me, and then very slowly placed the mug on the table. Scratching his chin, he stared out into the valley. Fronds of sunshine slipped through the olive canopy onto his face. One of the light spots stuck to the centre of his forehead like the dot of a question mark. "Could that...like...make a health problem? Never heard of someone crapping in a box before."

"It's the healthiest, cleanest, most environmentally-friendly way of creating a toilet. You mix your poo with sawdust and leave it for six months. Then it biodegrades and becomes harmless. After that you can use it on your garden." I smiled knowledgeably.

"You're gonna put your crap on your vegetables?" Celal peeled off his cap and scratched his scalp vigorously.

"Yes! It'll be amazing. You wait and see." I sprang from my stool exuberantly, itching to create this wonder of eco-engineering.

"'S alright, you don't have to show me," Celal said quickly, before easing himself onto his feet.

This was to be my first taste of the widespread horror, both local and international, circulating the concept of the composting toilet. Along with Portland cement, the composting toilet has become a pet campaign of mine. The global ignorance regarding the health and environmental impacts of mainstream sewage systems beggars belief at times. Mixing your poop with water is absolutely the *worst* thing you can do, because the pathogens and diseases in faeces need moisture to survive. To mitigate this, modern sewage systems construct expensive and fuel-hungry treatment plants. In countries with a less-developed infrastructure, like Turkey, that sewage is stored in leaky cesspits for *years* before finally being sucked out by a poop truck and then dumped in a forest.

But despite all this, according to the birdbrained logic of The World-At-Large, it is my dry composting toilet, a toilet that leaves no trace of its contents within six months, that is the health hazard. *Right.*

Now I have to admit, on this sunny June morning I was still very much a poop experimenter. I was riding on the turd-littered experience of an eco-farm friend of mine. She swore by her shit box. And it was so simple to make, I'd decided to give it a go. Now the only obstacle was, I literally didn't know how to bang a nail in. Nor saw a piece of wood. So Celal, albeit reluctant, was my only hope.

Truth be told, when it came to woodwork Celal and I weren't exactly a dream team. His eyesight was so poor he couldn't read off the measurements. I had no patience. And neither of us enjoyed fiddling about with the spirit level for too long. Which is probably why my first composting toilet took a day to complete and finished up pitched at such an angle I had to hang on to the edge every time I used it.

***

Celal and I convened at the top of the land. The sun had already set the sky aflame, and we were sweating.

"Okay, it's going to be a metre square and half a metre high," I instructed. "Erm...how do we do this? Hmm, let's cut the supporting 10-by-10s first."

Celal and I bent over a pile of wood I'd just purchased. "Right you are," Celal grabbed the hand saw, while I held the post down by kneeling on it. Of course you don't need 10-by-10s for a composting toilet. It's not as if you're going to tap dance on the thing. 5-by-10s are ample. But *I* didn't know that, did I?

Some wheezing, sweating, and a fair bit of sawdust later, we had our four supporting posts cut to size.

"Let's bang a ring of the 10-by-1s around the bottom first. That ought to keep it in place, won't it?"

"Aye, I'll cut 'em." Celal reached for one of the thin laminated planks.

"No you don't need to. The wood yard cut it to size for me."

Celal nodded in approval. It turned out to be one of my smarter decisions, as it saved us (or rather Celal) a lot of sawing. As the cutting work seemed to be over, Celal grabbed the posts, while I pulled out the planks, and we both headed for my 'bathroom'. It was a secluded space at the forest edge obscured from view by an olive tree and plenty of thorns bushes. It was also blissfully cool compared to the sun-ravaged crown of my land.

Squatting on a few rocks, I held the posts firm(ish) while Celal banged the planks onto them. The forest rustled as a light breeze played with its millions of pine needles. But everything else was silent, each creature no doubt running for cover as the hammer sent shockwaves through the land.

An hour into our shit-box mission we had completed a wonky square with four legs poking up. We both surveyed our workmanship. I wobbled the legs, then Celal wobbled them.

"What next?" I asked standing upright and pulling the peak of my cap down.

"Less get four more 10-by-1s and join the top up. Then it'll be a box, won't it?" Celal seemed a little more motivated now the structure was coming to life. I concurred, and gamely jogged up to the wood heap at the top of the land. It was a hot steep canter, the sweat collecting under my cap and around my neck with each step. Pulling my gardening gloves back on, I picked up four more planks and charged back down to the bathroom.

Once again, I held the planks to the posts while Celal whacked the nails home. Every hit reverberated through my body, until I wasn't sure whether it was me being hammered or the plank. Finally, he was done and the resembled a box, or at least a 3D drawing of a box. For it was all lines and no filling. Now all that remained was to render the construction level(ish). Sigh...

To this day this levelling roguery tries my patience. Well, it's so fiddly, isn't it? And it takes *such* an inordinate amount of time, far longer than the banging together of the structure. First you have to find all these darn rocks. Then you have to slide them one by one under the structure. But the worst bit is the measuring for levelness, and the laborious pulling out of one rock and replacing it with another until the structure sits straight.

"Ah, 's alright, innit? All you're gonna do is crap on it."

"Well, I don't know, Celal. I might read on it too."

Celal looked at the box, and then back at me, and then once more back at the box. I just *knew* my comment had generated too many images.

"Aye. Used to smoke when I was on the crapper, before I gave up."

"When did you stop smoking?" I turned to Celal in surprise.

"'Bout a year ago, cos me lungs were packing up on me. Doctor said if I didn't quit I'd be dead in a year. I was smokin' a hell of a lot, four packets a day."

My mouth fell open. *Four* packets. I quickly did the maths. That was eighty a day, so on the basis that Celal slept eight hours that meant eighty in sixteen hours, or five an hour... *Five* an hour? *Five*? He must have been chain-smoking non-stop from morning until night! No wonder his lungs were caving in on him.

I raised myself up on my haunches and studied Celal's scrawny little body. There wasn't an ounce of fat hiding anywhere on him. His face was a storybook of character lines. I could sense that story was a hard one.

"How old are you, Celal?"

"Fifty-nine. Be sixty this year."

I gazed at him, admiring his stamina for manual labour. At that point in the mud adventure, Celal could out-perform me a good five times over, and I was twenty years his junior. This balance of energy was to change over the next year or two, but nonetheless, Celal was fit. Back on that sunny May day did Celal have any inkling of the exploits and conquests ahead of us? Because there were so many unknowns lurking on the track ahead. Victories. Defeats. Births and deaths. We were to become the closest comrades in mud arms until the day he died.

The sun pushed through the spiked claws of the oak behind us dappling the scene. Celal threw the shit box a cursory stare. He stood over it, while I sat on a rock beginning to feel tired. We had both had enough of it and just wanted to bang the side panels on. Regarding the box dubiously, I shrugged in defeat.

"Giss a plank and I'll nail the bugger in place." Celal rocked on his heels with the hammer in his hand.

I pulled out a 10-by-1 and slid it across the top of the box. Then something occurred to me. *Yes*. Why not?

"Hey, Celal. Can I have a go at nailing? I've never done it before."

Celal sat back and grinned. Then he held out the hammer. "Yeah 's good to learn, innit? I'll hold the plank. Try and miss me hand, alright?"

I stretched my brow from my chin to indicate I'd do my very best. As Celal wrapped his hands around the plank, I marvelled at his bravery. You wouldn't have caught my hand anywhere near a nail anyone else was about to whack. Though of course if I'm the one with the hammer, I have to hold the nail, don't I? Carefully, I gripped the nail between my index finger and thumb and positioned it on the plank, lining it up with the one before. Then I tentatively brought the hammer down. It did nothing. The nail wobbled and fell out. I picked it up and tried again. This time I hit my thumb.

"Ow! Ooh ow ow! Oof. Ouch! *Shit*!"

Celal giggled as I hopped about sucking my red digit.

"Ah, 's all part of hammerin', that is. You'll get used to it. My thumbs don't feel nothing any more."

I stared at Celal wide-eyed, then stared at my thumb, sincerely hoping it wouldn't reach that stage.

Third time lucky. I positioned the nail, funnelled my concentration on the head and then tapped it. It held. Holding my breath, I smacked it a bit harder. Still good. Finally, I whacked it. It buckled in the centre.

"Oof! I'm hopeless. Look at that. Now what do we do?" I threw the hammer down in disgust.

Celal chuckled happily to himself. "We yank the bugger out, that's what. Giss the hammer. I'll show you." And he slid the nail into the hammer's groove and promptly extracted it. It dropped into the rocks like a mangled claw.

Eventually, after much swearing and the rising of a good many feelings of incompetence, I managed to bang a nail in. But it was clear, if I was to carry on, we'd be at this shit box until doomsday. Sighing, I handed Celal the hammer. Then I grabbed a plank and he set to banging in nails.

Five o'clock arrived. It was time for Celal to knock off. The sun was on the edge of losing power. And, happily for me, my first-ever composting toilet was complete. It was wonky, lurched backward into a thorn bush, and was facing the wrong way (I wanted a view!). But it was my first semi-successful architectural project, and I loved it.

I ran up the hill to my car and hurriedly unlocked the boot. Celal followed me. We both grabbed the large sack of sawdust inside by an end, and walked back with it to the bathroom to dump it on the back of the shit box. Celal opened the fraying mouth and peered tentatively inside.

"The sawdust is what you cover your crap with, so it doesn't smell," I explained.

Celal raised his eyebrows. "'S like a big cat tray, innit?" he said, and closed the sack.

I grinned at him, handed him the hammer and nails to carry up the hill, and we both made for the top of the land. When we reached the stubble-covered brow, Celal turned and faced the panorama. The valley was an erratic flow of green and brown, the mountains' peaks forming a crenelated rampart around it. And beyond that rocky fortress stretched the endless expanse of the sky. I saw the speck of a buzzard circling in the distance. It bobbed and glided in the limitless blue, searching for sustenance, free from the Earth and yet simultaneously tied it.

"So did yer start teaching your lesson thing down there?" Celal nodded in the direction of the Lost Valley. The early evening light had caught the dry riverbed from afar. It was a dusty brown serpent weaving between the mountains.

"Oh, don't even ask," I replied. A current of worry stirred in my belly. "It seems I'm not going to teach after all. So I'd better think of something else to live on, hadn't I?"

Celal brought his hand to his chin, a hand that had seen a good forty-five years of hard work. He scratched his whiskers. Then he moved his head forward. "Aye, you had," he said, before turning away from the view, and trudging off up the hill.

Creatures of the Night

The next few days passed uneventfully. June was here and the heat was rising. But though the countryside was opening into summer, I began a type of hibernation. Soon enough, I stopped descending into the valley and enclosed myself completely in my land. It was my cocoon. I watched swallowtail butterflies flutter onto thistles, gracefully flapping their webbed wings. I gazed at the dog roses, now shrivelling slightly. Praying mantis wobbled slowly as they moved from stalk to stalk. Everything knew exactly what it was doing. Nothing in nature seemed to be agonising over where it was supposed to go, or what it was supposed to be. There was no 'supposed to' for the grasshoppers and the tortoises. They just lived from their cores.

I wanted to do the same. Uncompromisingly. Unapologetically. I wanted to be real, to live from the marrow of my being. Work from it. Do nothing other than embody it. But what was the real me? Or the real you? Or the real any of us? And in this world of money and jobs and social expectation, could I possibly survive by embodying it?

"Here you are, my girl, I've brought you some frozen water. You can put it in your fridgebox thing and keep your cheese fresh." Dudu handed me a solid and transparent Coca Cola bottle over the fence. I grabbed it gratefully, feeling it stick to my hand.

"Ah thanks, Dudu. You're a star."

"We were the same, I told yer, me and me husband, God rest his soul. We moved up here in 2006 and planted this orchard. But he didn't even make it a year! Allah Allah! Now I'm stuck here on my own." Her face shrank into her headscarf as she spoke, small brown sun spots disappearing into the wrinkles. With her flowery şalwars rucked over her belly, she was a cockled dwarf.

"How did your husband die, Dudu?"

"Heart attack. Right here." She pointed to an area in the ditch only about five metres from my fence. I stifled a gulp.

"Was pruning the pomegranates, and just fell down he did. And that was that. Thank the Lord he didn't do it near *my* house, or I'd never go out again! Ooh, I don't want to see his ghost lurking about."

The light was already fading. I stared at the infamous spot in the ditch, and one by one each hair on my scalp stood up.

"Haven't you sprinkled that yet?" Dudu's voice was high-pitched with frustration. I snapped my gaze back to see her peering over the fence at the black plastic bag of sulphur I'd left under a bush. "Why haven't you spread it? What are you waiting for? You need to circle your tent with it now, my girl, or you'll have snakes and scorpions and all sorts of trouble."

I looked at the bag. It was spewing caustic yellow powder from its top. Why hadn't I used it yet? It was a good question.

And right there and then I heard a rustle in one of the old olive trees. It was followed by a soft scuffle. I blinked and inhaled slowly, because I knew who it was. Twisting my head around, I saw my dirt woman hunched on all fours over the bag like an overgrown furless cat. She eyed it ferociously, a low growl rumbling from her throat.

"Anyway, I'm going back before it gets dark," Dudu squawked, oblivious to my prehistoric landmate. She drew her headscarf a little tighter around her chin. "If you need anything, you know where I am. Oh, but you won't come, will you now? You *never* come to my house!" Then she swivelled around, and trotted off into the pomegranates, their spiny branches twitching in her wake.

I turned back to Dirt Woman. She was sniffing the sulphur bag warily, circling it as though someone had dropped a case of plutonium in front of her. Raising the nest of her head, she hurled me an intense glare. "You no use this. It hurt my friend," she said.

I squinted at her. *"Friend?"* Feeling an itch on my arm, I began to scratch. As far as I was concerned friends possessed between two and four legs, not more, not less.

Friends didn't stick their fangs into you, or send you to hospital in an ambulance. At least, *my* friends didn't.

"Are you saying snakes are my *friends*?" I walked closer to my dirtier sister, looking her up and down. Her brown legs were bent at the knee, and her arms hugged them. She rocked a little, clearly disgruntled.

"We all together. This our home. We all family!" she muttered to the sulphur bag.

"But...but snakes might bite me! They're dangerous!"

"Wheel machine more dangerous. But you no scared of it."

Placing my hands on my hips, I sighed. It was a fair point, but even so.

"Snake no much dangerous if you friend with her. If you stupid, she bite you. If you 'wake and listen her, she no bite you. If you show her your place she respect...Snake very..." Here the dirt woman paused searching for a word. She put a finger to her mouth, her black eyes rolling up into her lids. "Snake very senseeteev."

"Sensitive?"

Dirt Woman nodded. "And she very shy. She no want to see people." Here my friend from the mud opened her mouth and began to chortle. "Same like you," she guffawed.

I raised an eyebrow. This was the first time I'd ever entertained the possibility that I had anything in common with a snake.

Screwing up my forehead, I wondered what to do about the sulphur. I couldn't just leave it festering there under a bush. Should I throw it away? And then how would I protect myself from dangerous critters? It was all very well for Dirt Woman to say I should be awake and listen, but I was new out here. I didn't know how to communicate with creepy crawlies. Or how to show them my place. It was a dilemma.

Dirt Woman stood up and patted me on the shoulder. "It is day end. I find sleep place." She grinned and padded past me, butt as firm as fired clay. In one incredible bound, she had cleared the top ridge, and was scampering toward the fearsome forest.

Dusk was now a soup of grey so viscous even Dudu's pomegranate branches couldn't stir it. I blinked. The dinge seemed to sit on my lashes, and I strained my eyes against it. Still standing at the fence, I studied that space five metres away. The space where Mr Dudu had died. I imagined him there, secateurs in hand, clawing at his chest, before he sank onto his knees and into the ditch. *Didn't even make it a year.*

Suddenly, it occurred to me how strange it was that Dudu and I lived side by side. Two single women. It's highly unusual for *anyone* to live alone in Turkey. And women? As rare as an objective fact in a tabloid newspaper. In Turkey, women who are no longer married, are generally referred to as *dul*. The word literally means widow, but locals tend to call you that even if you're divorced. Both Dudu and I were *dul*. Had I known at that time there was a third *dul*, that we were three witches in a row, I'd have definitely sniffed something amiss.

Darkness began to pour into the fields. It seemed to rise from the ground up, as though the landscape was a boat with a leaky bottom. First the soil disappeared beneath the black ripples, then the trees. The ominous Mr-Dudu-eating ditch vanished beneath the surface. As night rose and reached my shoulders and my neck, I felt each notch of my spine turn cold.

I decided not to enter Dudu's land after dark. Who knew what I'd meet?

Turning swiftly, I galloped over to my tent. Kicking off my boots, I ripped open the zipper and threw myself inside, speedily shutting the hatch behind me. Feeling for the solar lantern, I flicked the switch. The tent shone with blue light, which only added to the phantasmal aura of the place. My toes scrunched up. My teeth dug into my gums. Oh dear. The heebie-jeebies were here. I just knew it was going to be one of those nights.

Wikipedia won't tell you this, nor will the *Oxford Dictionary*, but heebie-jeebies are tiny terror-spreading mites that crawl into your brain and eat out your common sense. They only come out at night. Usually at three in the morning. Sometimes though, they'll get you earlier. And once you're infested with them, they're horribly difficult to get rid of. Within minutes of laying down, I knew the heebies had got me. I also noted that Apo wasn't here.

Of course, what I *should* have done at this juncture was call upon Dirt Woman. Such night terrors were her domain, not the territory of a wayward modern whose only resource on such matters was *Friday the 13th* and *The Blair Witch Project*. All I could think to do was draw my knees up to my chin and cower inside my tent. Exactly how a flap of canvas was supposed protect me from the living dead, I have no idea. As I said, the heebie-jeebies had devoured my reason.

Perching on my sleeping bag, I reached out and touched the blue silk of the tent. It squeaked under my fingers. Looking about me, I spied my water bottle and a packet of crisps. I exhaled gratefully. This meant I wouldn't have to venture outside to find food. Holding the water bottle to my lips, I glugged. Then I opened the crisp packet. It made such a racket in the quiet of the night, they probably heard it over in Yapraklı village. Once the crisps were demolished, I pulled a book out. But it was a pointless exercise as I kept reading the same sentence over and over again. I couldn't focus. My ears were on alert. I was waiting to hear Mr Dudu's ghost. Would he call from over the fence? And what would he say if he did?

I'm glad he didn't die next to my house. Dudu's words hung inside the tent like cold, damp washing.

Eventually, I extinguished the light and decided to try and sleep, but every single cell within me was primed for trouble. The air inside the tent was pulled so taut I wasn't sure I could breathe it. And then the rustling began. Or was it a slithering? Or a scampering?

Unlike the night when Apo had turned up, this noise wasn't that of a large mammal. It was decidedly critterish. There was a slipping sound on the tarp. I flashed open my eyes. Was it inside or out? I gaped into the black. But it made no difference. The darkness was complete. There was no moon, not even a crescent, and my mind filled the absence with monstrous things. Whimpering a little, I reached for my torch, all the time terrified my hand would brush something. The plastic torch handle eventually fell under my hand, and I flicked the switch. Flashing the beam wildly about the tent, I searched for the phantom slitherer. Nothing. Nowhere. And no slithering now either.

I made a mental list of possible offenders. It read like the credits of a horror movie: whip snake, Ottoman viper, grass snake, scorpion, camel spider, huntsman spider, black widow. And then I remembered the sulphur I hadn't sprinkled.

Dropping back onto my bed, I turned the torch off again, now hugging it like a baby. The light hadn't been extinguished more than a minute before the slithering started once more. I flashed on the torch and lay stock-still. The slitherer did likewise.

"Fuck you!" I banged my hand on the canvas. The tent shuddered. Then nothing.

This routine went on for a good thirty minutes. I would turn off the torch. The slithering would start, sometimes behind me, sometimes above me. I'd turn on the light, try to find the slitherer and fail. Then I'd shout a few obscenities at it. But the slithering slider just didn't care.

And then of course, as always happens, I needed a pee.

I crossed my legs and tried to think about something else. Bolting my thighs together, I did my best to put off the moment of doom. I squirmed, turned this way and that. But it was futile. There was no way I'd last all night, and I knew it. I took a few deep breaths. They didn't erase the images of giant crab spiders and Ottoman vipers. Not to mention the secateurs-wielding ghost of Mr Dudu.

Emitting a few plaintive bleats, I girded my loins and reached for the zipper. Express trains of adrenalin were now charging over the biochemical rails of my body. It was then, because I couldn't stand being an ounce more afraid, that I opted for a junction switch change. Instead of sending my adrenalin to station fear, I shunted it over to the aggression dock. The tent flap ratcheted open. Then torch in hand, I stepped out into the darkness.

"Fuck off all of you horrible night things. *Fuck off!*" I bellowed, waving the torch about wildly. I threw the beam right. "Fuck off!" Then left. "Fuck you!" Before I scuttled to the side of the tent. Pulling down my pyjama bottoms I bopped, and then shrieked and leapt straight up again. Something had tickled my inner thigh. What? Agh! "Fuck off, fuck off, *fuck off!*"

Aggressive people are always scaredy-cats, the same way bullies are always cowards. I checked the area with my torch. A grass stalk poked jauntily out of the earth. This was the culprit, and I stamped on it furiously before squatting again. Men should be very happy they don't have to get their privates this close to the ground when they pee, that's all I can say. Never has a toilet mission seemed to take so long.

Shivering and shaking, I galloped back to the tent. I was just about to unzip the door when I saw it.

The Slitherer!

The Slitherer saw me too. Its small beady eyes stared up at me from the top of the tent canvas. Its reptile body was frozen in fright. This was the perpetrator of my insomnia. The gruesome monster of my nightmares...

It was a lizard. A gecko in fact. Tiny, web-footed, pink and harmless. The small reptile peered up at me petrified. I exhaled, feeling idiotic. Gecko and I gaped at each other for a moment or two, before I sank down and crawled back into the tent.

As I lay down on my sleeping bag, I began to wonder. Why was that gecko here? Why would any small lizard be so obsessed with my tent canvas, despite the fact it housed a foul-mouthed, torch-waving maniac. *Why?*

***

The next morning, I stepped out of my tent and stumbled into my make-shift 'kitchen'. I gawped bleary-eyed at the ramshackle washing-up stand and my washing-up bowl and stray pots. Something struck me. As I glanced about, I realised. There were no crumbs anywhere, no leftovers to clean up. In short, no mess at all.

It took a few moments for me to completely register it. But as I picked up the saucepan I'd cooked a tomato sauce in the night before, and stared at the cleaned inside, the penny dropped. My leftovers were other animals' feasts.

As I poured a tightly rationed bowl of water from the canister and began washing the already clean pan, I began to smile. Gecko was doing me a favour here. As were the skinks, the mice, and the cats. As I flicked the sponge around the stainless steel bottom, I finally saw the larger picture. We were all doing each other a favour. This land wasn't a bunch of isolated individuals out to get each other. We were one integrated tribe. The creatures of the night enjoyed free food. I received polished saucepans. The trees sucked in my CO_2, and I inhaled their oxygen.

I was rough around the edges in those days, so these simple equations were my way of understanding. But in truth, logic is nothing but a rudimentary net the human mind casts over the wild intelligence of nature. Beneath and beyond concepts of symbiosis and mutual profit campaigns lies mystery. Because the tribe of my land worked in incredible ways. Ways at that time I simply couldn't imagine. Ways that defied anything I'd ever been taught about life and co-existence.

Liquid Diamonds

"So, can I have a water connection then?"

I was down in the valley, supping a glass of tea with the village headman. We were opposite each other on a wooden table. He was scratching the silver hair on his head and refusing to look me in the eye.

"We're not giving permission for water connections any more. You'll have to go to the borough."

"They said I need a power connection before I can have a water connection."

The man shrugged and began picking something out of his teeth.

"And I can't get a power connection without your permission either," I continued, staring him square in the face.

"Then you can't have water," the headman replied. He studied the shred of sunflower seed he'd dislodged from his gums before flicking it onto the ground. I briefly entertained a fantasy of grabbing him by the collar and head-butting him. In my mind's eye, I watched his head rock back and forward like an egg on a worktop, which made me feel ever so slightly vindicated. I took a deep breath.

"But everyone says, if you give me a special piece of paper I *can* get a water connection! And you've given it to plenty of other people." I put both my hands palms down on the table between us and proffered him a beseeching look. We'd known each other a few years, so I was presuming he'd cut me a little slack here.

"I told you, we're not giving permission any more. You'll have to get water from elsewhere. Tap into your neighbour's pipe."

"But that's illegal! She won't give it to me, I've already asked."

He shrugged again and exhaled in boredom. "Can't help you then," he said and stood up.

I felt the anger rising from my solar plexus into my chest. Taking to my feet, I tersely shook the headman's hand. *Fine. Just fine. I will indeed get water from somewhere else. I'll be independent, never have to kiss your arse, and there'll be nothing you can do about it.*

I don't suppose the headman ever knew the impact his unhelpfulness would have upon me. But it was in fact this conversation that fuelled my rejection of The System. It was a forced rejection. As I have often said, obstacles nearly always turn out to be our friends, pushing us from one destiny and into another. In my case, this new destiny was going to be off-grid, legislation-ignoring, and free. I had never intended it. I'd never even considered it until that moment to be honest. And it wasn't going to come without a price, either. Because living without running water is tough. Very tough.

With a small and now-grotty daypack on my back, I ambled up the dirt road of the Lost City and toward Café Cactus. My rucksack pulled on my shoulders. I'd collected a few beach pebbles in it, and it clanked as I walked.

The riverbed that ran beside the track had dried out and I gaped at the dusty trough of rocks. There would be no rain for a good four months. Water. I needed water. But how?

"The chief wouldn't give me a water connection." I slumped into a chair in Nilay's shop and began fiddling with her beads. Evren was perched on a chair opposite.

"Arsehole! If you were a local, he'd give you one just like that! He's saved all those permissions for his aunt's wife's brother, or some other inbred relative of his." Evren turned his head and scowled. His moustache had now grown so large it almost covered the lower half of his face. It was an entity in its own right. A brown, hairy, lip-squatting caterpillar.

"You can't live up there without water, Kerry! No, that really *is* impossible." Nilay held a cigarette to her lips and sucked on it. She was wearing a red scarf tied round her hair and large gold hoops in her ears, every bit the gypsy belle.

"I'm thinking of pumping it up from the canal," I said.

"But that water isn't clean!"

"I could filter it somehow. I heard someone set up a plant pond to filter it in and then used the water in a swimming pool."

Nilay's features shifted away from each other doubtfully. "What about drinking water?"

"Oh, that's not such a big deal. I can bring that in if need be. It's the other stuff, washing, watering plants, that's where I need a supply."

"Ah, there'll be a way. There's always a way. You might have a wellspring up there." Evren raised his finger and thumb to the centre of his caterpillar moustache and then parted them so they slid to its head and tail. "And the chief might still give you permission if you bribe him. That's what happened with Musti and Sevgi. Took them a year, they built the house, and then he gave in."

I straightened my back and pushed my chin out. Then I folded my arms. "No. I'll never ask him again. I'm not pandering to him. I shall get my own water and be free. That'll show him." A defiant smirk settled itself into my face, and it was obvious it planned on making itself comfortable.

"Ooh, Kerry, you're so stubborn. You're a Capricorn of course, that's why." Nilay shook her head, the gold rings in her ears twinkling. Evren's nostrils flared ever so slightly. He pursed his lips and said nothing.

"Evren, you know you said you could help me with my tent shade?" I perched on my chair and moved my torso in his direction. He blanched, suddenly becoming fascinated by the floorboards.

"Well, we're nearing mid-June. Do you think you could come up some time this week?" I wriggled and writhed in favour-asker agony, loathing the need for assistance.

"Yeah, yeah, just give us a ring when you're ready," he said, and waved his hand vaguely in the air.

***

That evening, I drove from the Lost City, along the winding road, past the mosque and the fire station. The switchbacks sucked me out of the valley and up to Yapraklı village. Pine forests fell over the mountainsides like woody rain. With their plunging roots the red pine could survive months without water.

Pulling over at the graveyard, I opened the back door of the car. I dragged out the two twenty-litre canisters wedged between the back and front seats. Setting the canisters beneath the spigots, I turned the taps. As I stood watching the water gush in, I became lost in the flow, the sparkling beauty of it. Water. It was now liquid diamonds to me. Once the tanks were full, I turned the plastic wheels of their lids and made sure they were shut fast. Finally, I heaved them up, one by one, and staggered with them to the open car door.

Huffing and groaning, I dropped the water tanks into place. There had to be a better way than this. There just *had* to be.

Soon I was back on my land. Dusk was falling. It was a magic mist. I stood at the edge of the wall and stared over my queendom. The rocks were glimmering again, their lines now silver. The remaining green splodges on the land began to turn luminous and my eye wandered from shrub to shrub. Most of the hill was now yellow, except for a few patches of green here and there. One of those patches was located at the lower west side of the land. In fact, that area was predominantly green, and mainly populated with myrtle bushes.

I wandered over to Grandmother Olive and stretched my hand out. Her trunk was, as always, warm to touch.

"Where's the water?" I asked.

This time, however, the tree was quiet. No words fell into me. But I did feel something else. I think I'd call it a sort of aesthetic pull by the land. Instinct and intuition were both coming alive.

Trotting to the right, I hopped past the olive tree and studied the dry gulch which Dudu said would turn into a stream in the winter. Putting my feet inside it, I followed the rocky path down. As the first star blinked overhead, I reached the end of the dry ditch. I was now positioned within the tract of green I'd spied from the top of the wall.

Standing in that lower, most-sheltered corner, the first thing I noticed was that it was markedly cooler here. The second was that there was plenty of vegetation about, whereas it had all shrivelled up and died elsewhere. I turned round and round in that space. It was invisible from everywhere else. A secret world.

As I inhaled the fresh air, I wondered. Could there be water below me?

My eyes turned back to the slope. I was looking up the hill, the dry grass now a thick golden pelt on the back of my land. All around the edge of the land, from the fearsome forest to Grandmother Olive and her sisters, trees began to sway. Gently. Very gently. And I sensed it. The magic. The wonder. The anything-is-possible holes yawning apart in the time-space continuum.

"Where does imagination come from? Have you ever wondered?" The trees whispered huskily into my ear. All of them. A chorus.

"I don't know where it comes from. But it feels good. It feels free and alive. And on this land it feels...inspired."

Closing my eyes, I inhaled. The evening musk of the land entered my nostrils and moved into my lungs. "Inspired. From the French, *inspirer*. And the Latin *inspirare*. To breathe in," I heard myself say. "And it feels like that. As though the land, or something in it, is breathing ideas into my mind and soul. But it's not like when the television or internet fills my head. This feels..."

A balmy wave of air washed over my face and shoulders.

"It feels *divine*. There are so many possibilities. So many pathways. As though my brain has been watered and is sprouting thousands of new shoots. I have no idea if the land is speaking to me or if I'm creating the thoughts, or if it's some combination of the two. But either way, it's beautiful. Joyful."

The breeze picked up and rushed through the trees, shaking their woody arms. It fanned the grass stalks, just as it played with my hair. The last pearls of daylight evaporated one by one, turning the land into a tenebrous mystery.

Heading back up the hill, I retraced my footsteps along the gulch. The rocks were still a shade lighter than anything else, so the path was slightly illuminated. When I reached Grandmother Olive, I put my hand on her crusty trunk. Darkness was everywhere now. But I felt no fear. A sing-song trilling began to emanate from the forest. The cicadas were quiet. It was the turn of the crickets now. As their vibrato became louder I turned to face the slope suddenly knowing this water thing would resolve itself. Because this was *my* land. Mine. Mine! And she would take care of me. We would take care of each other.

It was then I saw the dark outline of Dirt Woman standing as solid as a thousand-year-old pine. She was positioned by a rickety wooden table I'd just acquired, poring over the beach stones I'd collected earlier in the day.

"Oh, so *beautiful!*" she whispered, picking up one that looked like an ostrich-egg and clutching it to her breast. "So beautiful!"

I scuttled next to her and grinned. "Yes. Yes, they are."

Both of us stood there looking from the stones to each other, the same idea forming in our minds at exactly the same time.

"Look, iss tree! The rock all have story in!" My ancestor gripped my bicep. Pulling me closer to her face, she stared into my eyes in that unnerving, far-reaching way of hers. Her dreadlocks formed a mane and she was a dusky lion in the darkness. And I was suddenly filled with a powerful urge to paint. To tell the story of the stones.

***

I began the next day. And continued the next. And the next. Hunched over my table, I would pull a rune toward me. I had no plan of what to paint. No image I wanted to impress upon it. Randomly, I would dip a small brush in a pot. A wave of something beautiful would fill me. The brush would glide over the face of the stone, swirling this way and that as if possessed.

And the thing I loved painting above all else was trees with their coiling serpent arms. They were moving so slowly my eyes couldn't pick up their dance. But something else inside me could see it. The woody, sap-filled ballet of the forest. A choreographed wonder that a human mind could normally only observe via a time-lapse camera.

One evening, as dusk threaded its way through the forest and moved steadily up my land, I gathered a clutch of my painted stones. One by one I positioned them in the craters of an egg-box. Then I placed them on the passenger seat, and drove down to the valley, to Nilay's jewellery store.

"Here you go!" Gently I held the egg-box up to Nilay with a reverence more appropriate for the crown jewels. She picked up a blue one with an orange fish on it. Then one with a black tree on a red and orange background. Slowly she turned them over and smiled.

"Oh, they're *lovely!* Let's put them here." She pointed to a space on one of her jewellery cabinets. I puffed up in newbie artist pride.

"Sooo..." She crossed her legs, put her hands on her knees, and batted her eyelids at me cheekily. "How much do you want for them?"

I shuffled on my seat. "Oh, I don't know. How much do you think they're worth?" I asked coyly, still eyeing them possessively from my chair. Nilay snickered. She picked up a smaller one and turned it over thoughtfully.

"Five lira for the small ones, ten for the medium-sized ones, and fifteen for the larger ones, what do you say?" Then she pulled out a pen and some stickers from a drawer under her white desk and handed them to me. "Here you go, price them up!"

Over the following weeks, to my amazement my stones began to sell. True, *Forbes* magazine wasn't exactly ringing my phone off the hook for an interview. I probably earned about $30-$40 a week from my efforts. But up here in my new world it was enough to survive.

The Living Carpet

It was June. I had survived a month. And it showed. There was now a crust of dirt permanently lodged under my fingernails, my face had been grilled deep brown, there were tangles in my hair I could no longer brush out, and I was wearing the same clothes for a week at a time. Even Dirt Woman was impressed.

The land had also changed. In April it had been a meadow of lush green grass and flowers. In May the grass had turned yellow. By June, it had broken into a morass of burrs and thorns. Burrs are a phenomenon of great genius. Grasses use them to spread their progeny by hitchhiking lifts in mammalian fur or within birds' feathers. Unfortunately, they also have a penchant for human socks.

A type of routine had now emerged within my new outdoor life. I'd wake up at dawn with sparrows twittering maniacally about me, the cheeks of the sky flushing new born pink. Next I'd throw on my clothes and jump, yes *jump,* out of the tent because dawn was so inspiring I didn't want to miss it. I'd jam my feet into my fast-disintegrating hiking boots, and trot over to a large kilim folded up on the ground. Opening the Turkish rug, I'd stretch and meditate for an hour, before folding the mat up, pushing my feet into my boots again, at which point I'd wander past the leaking bag of sulphur I'd moved to the back of the tent. Every day, a thought would slide along the conveyor belt of my mind. *Should I spread a ring of that around my tent today?* And every day I'd see an image of a shrivelled reptile, then suffer a pang of premonitory guilt. The sulphur remained in its bag. Until one morning, something happened that determined its fate once and for all.

***

It was a gusty incinerator of a day. The type of day where you can't make up your mind whether to open the car windows and be grilled to death, or close them and boil instead. I was careering back from the city of Antalya with three rolls of bamboo matting attached to my roof rack. The matting stretched all the way from the bonnet to the rear bumper, and I could see it bounce whenever I drove over a ridge. Every time I braked, the matting inched forward, so I was anxious to vacate the main road a) before the matting shot off the front of the car, and b) before a traffic policeman in search of a bribe pulled me over.

It was just as the road began to thin and Mount Olympos rose into view that I remembered something. I'd forgotten to fold up my yoga rug...

By the time I returned to the land, it was late afternoon. I trudged onto the plot, a huge roll of bamboo matting seesawing on my shoulder. I was preparing for my first large construction project: a proper tent shade. As I approached my tent, I spied my yoga rug stretched open in the middle of the scrub with the wind blowing heartily across it. Had I possessed a free hand, I would have slapped my forehead. Before I even approached the kilim, I knew what I would see: burrs, there would be hundreds of them, all over it. And once in, those spikes would never come out.

Walking to the back of the tent, I dropped the roll of bamboo onto a sheet of plastic. Standing back up, I ambled over to the yoga rug. Then I scowled. *Agh!* Sure enough, the green and red weave was now spattered with arrows of dry grass. They were burrowing into it as though hunting for gold. I stamped my foot and cursed, neither of which helped.

Kneeling on the edge of the carpet, I lifted my sunglasses and peered at the spiky nodules. I yanked one of them. It broke off, leaving the head embedded in the rug like a tick in a dog's ear. I sighed. It was hopeless.

I decided to abandon the kilim. My knees creaked a little as I stood up. I wandered back to the car. Then I continued unloading bamboo matting thinking no more about it.

Little did I know my land was hatching something. Something that would change the way I viewed *everything*. Forever.

***

The next morning, I followed my usual morning routine. First I headed for my bathroom, which by now was state-of-the-art. It had an entrance with an old curtain attached to an arch of branches. Beyond the curtain was a cubby hole in the forest surrounded by prickly oaks and thorn bushes. In one corner squatted the composting toilet. In the other, I'd fastened a hose to a small plastic tank and perched it on a boulder above. This was my shower. I'd covered the 'floor' in small rocks to prevent the area from becoming muddy. There was even a mirror that Nilay had given me dangling from an olive branch.

As the sun shimmied through the pine branches, I stepped out of the bathroom and trod up the slope to my yoga kilim. It was then I remembered. *Shit*! Because of the burrs, the mat was useless, wasn't it? I walked over to it, intending to bunch it up and relegate it to some dirtier purpose. However, when I reached its edge, I stopped mid-step. Then I gasped.

The kilim was alive.

On first sight it was the stuff of nightmares. My stomach shrank from the edges of my abdomen, and I put my hand to my mouth. Because the carpet had become a sea of large, black ants. Yes! There was now a terrible orgy of these insects cavorting amidst the grass and burrs and other debris.

Good grief! What was I supposed to do now? It was early, and I'm a grumpy old hag before coffee. I turned and loped back to the tent, passing the sulphur bag yet again. It caught my eye. I stopped. Specks of yellow powder were visible through the opening of the bag. Picking the black plastic sack up, I walked back to the kilim with an intent that wasn't particularly nature-loving.

Perhaps I did need poison. I mean, a gecko here and there was one thing, but ant infestations? Scorpions? Snakes? I needed to face the face that sometimes my Dirt Woman was wrong. Yes, I'd sprinkle a ring of sulphur around my tent, and then another ring where I wanted my yoga kilim to be. I had a right to my own territory, after all. The critters could have the rest of the land. *This* part was mine.

And here we see the human issue: despite all these wonderful insights, down here on the ground I hadn't in fact digested the fact that we were all now one tribe. On a practical level I was still acting as though we were separate, with individual agendas and unrelated needs. But my land had a surprise in store for me.

Just as I was holding the plastic bag, and staring appalled at the hub of six-legged activity my kilim had become, I spotted something. Something unbelievable. The sulphur bag fell from my grip and hit the dirt with a small thud. Moving closer to the rug, I sank into a squat. No. It simply couldn't be true! I blinked. And blinked again. A wave of emotion crashed within me. The salty surf filled my throat and my eyes. It paralysed me. You see, the ants were carrying something on their backs: burrs.

To this very day the memory of this incident affects me. To this very day I am awed.

My lower jaw fell open. I watched in stupefaction as these tiny insects yanked and struggled and hauled great tufts of dry grass from the rug, and then gamely wandered off onto the ant highway with their cargo. I followed the ant road with my eyes, wondering where they were taking the burrs, and what they could possibly want with them. I would never learn that. It was yet another of nature's mysteries.

With a lump in my throat, I stood up. Without a moment's thought, I picked up the bag of sulphur, walked with it to my rubbish pile, and lobbed it into the waste ready to be transported out on my next trip to a city.

***

That evening, just before twilight hit the land, I checked on the yoga kilim. There wasn't an ant to be seen. Nor a burr. Nor a tuft of grass. It was spotless. My skin puckered into goosebumps at the sight of it. My eyes stung. And then gratitude surged through my entire being with such force I felt giddy.

As dusk cast his silver nets over the land, I stared out into the valley. And I felt Dirt Woman beside me. A silence settled between us. It was a palpable presence. I gazed at the star agama on her shoulder. It hunched there like a pet budgie, small dragon-head raised, tongue stabbing the air for mosquitos.

"We your friend. I say you before. This home," said my ancient sidekick. I watched the dragon head of the agama nuzzle into her hair.

And for the first time, I truly understood it. The full extent of it. I thought about the geckos and my cleaned pots and plates, my guardian Apo, the carpet-cleaning ants. It wasn't some Disney fairy tale. This was real. I was seeing it with my very own eyes.

The creatures and plants of this planet respond to us. To our touch. Our thoughts and our emotions. To our pheromones, our energy field. They sense our intention. It's obvious once you think about it, once you shelve a lifetime of education inculcating we are somehow separate from the rest of nature, above it, superior, that insects possess no consciousness because...erm, they're small? That animals don't feel pain because...because we eat them and to admit that is ethically inconvenient?

Later I would read articles and books on this subject, and nod or shake my head depending on the interpretation. Monkeys have outperformed university students on memory tests (tests designed by humans for humans)[4], fish use tools[5], and the videos of crows solving multi-step logic puzzles have been watched by millions.

---

[4] **Chimpanzee Choice Rates in Competitive Games Match Equilibrium Game Theory Predictions**, Christopher Flynn Martin, Rahul Bhui, Peter Bossaerts, Tetsuro Matsuzawa, Colin Camerer, Published in Scientific Reports, 5 June 2014.
[5] **The Use of Tools by Wrasses (Labridae).** G. Bernardi in *Coral Reefs*, Vol. 31, No. 1, page 39; March 2012.

The anthropocentric attitude toward the natural world adopted by both science *and* religion is quite amazing when you look at it. It's a non-stop attempt to denigrate and subjugate it. It makes you wonder what humanity been so afraid of. Well, we know what it's afraid of. Not being top dog.

But in truth it's intuitive. Life on Earth is an all-communicating intelligence. If it wasn't, then how could we have evolved here? We are part of it.

There was, however, one question that remained unanswered in my mind. I turned to Dirt Woman. She looked peaceful, her features open and soft.

"So why doesn't this happen to everyone? All the time? I mean, people can have trouble with insects. Ants infest their homes, get in their sugar pots, sometimes they sting."

"This *our* land. You speak to it. It speak to you. You listen it. It listen you."

"So it's about creating a special space? About committing to it?"

Dirt Woman screwed up her nose. "Commmitt?"

"Commit is something you do in relationships. Friendships. Family. You make a decision and a promise to stay for the long-term, to fight for it, to protect it, and love it even if the going gets tough."

"Maybe. But you talk with land. You listen me and no throw the bad yellow thing. Ant know. Dog know. Bird know. Lizard know. They not stupid. They all watch you. They know your...your enerjee. Shining human is good for land, make more beauty, bring water and food. Everything grow more with shining human. They want you stay."

"Shining human?"

"You now shining little bit." The dirt woman's face cracked apart like a walnut shell to reveal a fabulous beam.

"What do you mean?"

"This a story. You want story of shining human?"

123

I hunched up my knees and gawped at the dirt woman intrigued. I'd never seen her as much of a raconteur. She barely had a grip on the past tense. "Okay..." I said, and waited.

Dirt Woman's gaze settled on the pine trees to her left. She uncrossed her bare legs, crossed them again. There was a loud hacking sound as she coughed up her usual throatful of spit and ejected it into the dust a metre in front of her. Finally, having prepared herself, she began.

"The forest was very big. So big. Like a *world*. The trees was six, seven trees high. So high they touch the big Sky Spirit which hold all ideas; shining and dirty, true and trick. The rivers was full of diamond water then. So clean. All was clean. So many animals was here. So many flowers and plants. Verrrry beautiful. And humans was all shining then."

"Shining," I repeated.

"Yes. Shining. When they walk in the forest, all the trees love the human light and their leaves turn little bit when they see them. Because they look like sun. And humans was happy because they know forest is home and sky is all open and free."

I raised an eyebrow, but Dirt Woman saw nothing of it. She was deep in the time of the shining human.

"Then one day something fall from big Sky Spirit. It fly like the white black bird that steal thing."

"Like a magpie?"

"Yes. Like maggp-eye...The idea fly like maggp-eye to one human, and drop near to him. This human see new idea, he look at it. He listen it."

"What was the idea?"

"It says, *you different. You more clever than all other one. You can have control on the tree and animal.*"

"Ah...so it was a trick idea?"

"Big trick. And for a so-short time shining human shine a bit more, because he feel better than all world. But only a short time. Then very quick he feel bad. Because if he be more clever and different than all other thing in world, then he be all alone. A little bit dark come into human then, and it take away a little bit shine. The dark like a door in human soul, and all the many dark idea and trick in the Big Sky see it. Soon they all fly down like maggp-eye. They fly into human through that dark door. Slowly slowly human get very dark and the shining get less. His eye and mind get all dirty. He no see beauty and family and home. He no see love and true thing. Human get very lost. Very sad. Very angry. Very very scaredy-waredy. He make many thing for control world because he think he more clever, but he never control it, because it no true. He no more clever. He no different. It is a trick. He make this thing and that thing. But problem never stop. One machine stop one problem and it make ten more problem. He cut all tree and make all river dirty. He see animal and wild things like an...an...enemy. He kill them. He take all their food so they hungry and take his food. They sting him. They bite him. They no trust him now."

The dirt woman stopped here. Night was spilling into the land. It had already demolished the outlines of the trees. I could still just about make out my friend's face, her eyes glistening. But the darkness was eating into her too. It was eating into all of us.

"So the ants eat people's sugar in normal houses, because they have nothing else to eat. The balance of the ecosystem has been destroyed. Oh God, it's awful! It's hopeless!" I said, utterly forlorn.

But then Dirt Woman's face began to glow slightly. Her cheeks and chin appeared. I tilted my head up to see the yin-yang of a perfect half-moon rising over the forest.

"Yes. It look very bad," she said. "But look. You only here one month and you shining now. Human can change very quick. And if human change and begin shining, all world can change so so quick. All animal and tree waiting. Like ant and lizard here. They just waiting for shining human again."

The light of the half-moon slid through the valley, dusting it silver. The colossal peaks of the mountains reappeared. And I noticed just as day has its shadows, night always has its light. And that the Earth, no matter how it may appear to us now in our disassociated state, is a miracle.

The Secret Society

"Okay, I've got the lads. And the posts. And the bamboo. So when can you come?"

It had come to this. I was squeezing the favour out of Evren now. His voice rasped wearily back at me through the phone, "Alright. I'll be there about one."

I pressed the red button, and threw the phone back into my tent. I knew Evren didn't want to drag himself up here and build a tent shade. He had a thousand and one better things to do than oversee my project. The trouble was, I had no idea how to put together anything larger than myself, no experience of such a thing. And let me tell you, eking out experience is no mean feat with the Secret Society around.

The world of construction is much like the Freemasons (come to think of it, they started out as builders too), with secret handshakes, nods, and winks. If you happen to be the 'wrong' shape, size, or gender, few are those who will let you in, or share their knowledge with you. Answers are vague, hand tools are locked away, and you are generally shunted to one side and regarded as hopeless.

Now, I'll freely admit, I hadn't cared much about this exclusion in the past, because I had never possessed a smidgen of interest in construction. But two things had transpired in the past month to alter this attitude: 1. I was halfway up a mountain where structures were required, and I had no money to hire anyone to do it. 2. After my forays into washing-up racks and composting toilets, the building bug had begun to worm its way into me. I loved the sensation of creating things out of nothing, and a little builder ambition had sprouted. This was why I badgered Evren. The tent shade was my one shot at learning. I was going to study the construction assiduously, thereby gleaning arcane knowledge of the secret science of structure.

Though it was only a little past nine, the sun was already searing what was left of the grass stalks. A hint of cool still lingered in the air, but it was a frail reminder of night and losing territory fast. All three of us had scooted to the shadier west side of the land. It had been something of a mission to gather the team. Celal was on his way. I'd driven down to the valley to pick up the Cactus workers, both of whom had been fast asleep. They were now assembled on my land looking far from energetic. One of them, a shaggy-haired bartender was sprawled face down under Grandmother Olive, snoring. The other was a giant of a fellow called Deniz. He was sweating and wheezing just from the walk from my car.

"Mornin' all. Ah, we've got comp'ny today I see, that'll speed things up a bit, won't it?" Celal waved from the other side of the fence, his face crinkling under his baseball cap.

I was already beginning to sense it might not speed things up at all, but grinned up at him nonetheless. "Yes, and another friend is coming later to show us how to make a big shade for the tent," I waved him to join us. He wandered round the back of the property, behind the border of thorn bushes, and skipped up to us. He was trailed as usual by the trusty Apo.

Naturally, Apo bounded over to the one man standing. Deniz, alarmed, flapped his enormous arms up and down, and squawked. This only excited the Anatolian shepherd, who assumed this tower of a human wanted to play with him. Celal intervened and dragged Apo back. The dog shook his thick coat and trotted over to the olive tree, flopping down next to the shaggy-haired lad. This was altogether a helpful move, because it woke him up.

"Right, we need some rocks. While we're waiting for Evren, you can make a terrace over there with Celal," I said to the awakening bartender. With his round glasses, long hair and beard, he was John Lennon's Turkish doppelganger. He twitched. His head rolled slowly in my direction, the beard cracked apart and a long decisive yawn rolled out. "Oof, alright. Just a minute." Then a brown arm stretched out from under his half-naked body, a viper creeping out of hibernation. The hand fumbled for the spectacles.

"And *you* can help me gather some nice big rocks in the wheelbarrow," I said turning to giant Deniz.

"Hmph. It's hot. It's really hot."

"I know, but it's only going to get hotter." Already I could feel exasperation mounting inside me. *Come on, guys, give me a break, just help me out here for an hour or two.* "Look, we'll just do this bit and then we'll have a tea break, eh?" I bargained.

Celal stood in a corner surveying our new work team and chewing a piece of grass. He said nothing. He didn't have to.

Grabbing the blue handles of the barrow, I began walking. Deniz followed me, complaining all the way. He moaned about the heat, and the insects. And most of all the burrs.

"Ow! I keep getting spikes in my sandals, slow *down*."

I turned, barrow in hand, to see him stamping his foot on a rock. With his round face and rotund belly, he was a type of red Shrek. A dank pool of futility made its presence known somewhere inside me. Why was it always like this? I'd had plenty of experience working with 'volunteers' in the past. Some are angels. Others? You'd be better off strapping a couple of lead weights to your ankles and hiking across the Gobi than endure their 'help'. Because it wasn't coming for free. Nothing ever is. I was going to have to cook everyone lunch, and buy them beers. As I stood looking up at Deniz, I began calculating the cost and effort of him and the bartender. In about three seconds it became evident that someone like Celal – reliable, hard-working, honest, and needing neither transportation nor food because he lived next door, was worth his weight in gold.

The heat beat the top of my head. The pines roared with crickets. I tried to think of a job that Deniz would excel at. He was big. That had to mean brute strength, right?

"Hey, maybe you can pick up some monster rocks. They're too heavy for me. Like this one." I pointed at a nice fat boulder. Deniz puffed and spluttered as he approached. He glanced at the rock and smiled. Bracing his knees, he bent down. There was grunting. Then a groan. And finally a heavy clunk. I turned back round to see the rock in the barrow. Phew! One down, fifty more to go.

Deniz and I both collected rocks until the barrow was full. His success with the job motivated both him and myself. Now all we had to do was trundle the wheelbarrow back down to the land, to Celal and John Lennon, who I hoped was by now at least seventy per cent conscious.

"I can push it," said Deniz with gusto.

"Thank God for that!" I said, and made to pat him on the back, but found I couldn't reach. Stretching up on tiptoe, I managed to clap him on the scapula. He grinned and grabbed the metal handles, upon which his face contorted into an array of quite incredible expressions. Next he staggered forward with the barrow. It bumped over rocks and stones, clanking and wobbling.

Deniz managed to push the metal cart halfway down the slope, before yelping and releasing the handles. The barrow crashed to the ground. "Ow! Ooh, I *hate* these things. I hate them! Ow!" He was hopping about, his right foot in his hand, whimpering. Another burr attack. I sighed. Very slowly. Very deliberately. It was going to be a long, patience-sapping morning, and there was nothing to be done about it. I just had to suck it up, because the bottom line was they were 'doing me a favour'.

Deniz and I completed two barrow runs before he collapsed under the olive tree next to Apo. Guzzling a pint of water, he stretched out and moaned. Midday was here. The sun had positioned itself directly above and was funnelling fire onto the land. The grass shrivelled into weak patches. The faces of the pines became thickset as they braced themselves against the heat. But Grandmother Olive stretched upward, green, lush, and unperturbed.

Under her boughs, Celal and Bartender Lennon's terrace was rising. I noticed Celal throwing the odd disapproving glance at the younger man's bare chest. Rural folk don't think too much of nakedness, be it male or female. Even so, despite the culture gap, the two of them seemed to be getting on well enough. But I could see they needed more rocks. I collected and barrowed two more loads, while volunteer Deniz fanned himself in the shade.

Returning from my final rock-ferrying journey, I assessed the wall. It was gorgeously rustic. Celal had an intuitive way with rocks. For him a stone wall was a large three dimensional puzzle, and Bartender Lennon was learning from him. He too was hitting his stride now that afternoon was upon us. He stood up, bare torso gleaming with sweat. Running a hand through his curly brown locks, he smiled at me. "Ah, I only went to bed at five. I'm a night owl, and don't really come alive until evening."

Celal fixed his lips into a tight line. Deniz didn't even bother to hide his disgust. He shot the bartender a look of pure hatred, who in return shamelessly and openly smirked at him. I did my best to remain expressionless, but no doubt failed, because I have one of those faces that belies even the tiniest emotions. In the end, I decided the best thing to do was to evacuate the simmering triangle of testosterone and begin cooking lunch.

It was well past two in the afternoon when Evren arrived. The posts had been painted by me, and screwed together by Deniz, Bartender Lennon, and Celal. As Evren slammed his van door and galloped round the corner, past the dried-up dog roses and down the slope, I could see his face was set into a scaffold of exasperation. I empathised. A little. But I had to learn this wood business. Once and for all. It was my survival.

Walking round the posts, Evren gave them a cursory once over, his moustache pinching into a scowl.

"No, we can't put them up like this. You'll have to unscrew the lot of them."

I closed my eyes and counted a long way past ten.

Deniz brandished the drill. He was now a shiny mountain of sunburned flesh with a knotted handkerchief sitting atop his head. One by one he unscrewed the posts while I plied Evren with questions, trying to work out plan. The answers drifted back at me in ill-defined clumps. It was all so familiar. Perhaps he just didn't comprehend why I was asking. Perhaps it was simply too hot for explanations.

It didn't escape my notice that Deniz and John Lennon had sprung to attentive action once Evren had appeared. They both stood obediently holding posts, waiting for orders. "We need some flat rocks to wedge under the posts. First we'll stick 'em in, and prop 'em up. Then we'll fix the 5-by-10s across the top. And after that we'll set the posts straight." The instructions were directed over my head to Deniz. I inhaled. I exhaled.

Then I noticed something. Someone. A piece of me that didn't seem very 'nice'. The witch in me was cackling. I could feel her stretching into my body to the tune of "Right, like *that,* is it?" And what I realised was, I no longer cared.

"You've got a spirit level, haven't you?" Evren was now perched on a ladder that Celal was holding steady. He clutched a 10-by-10 in one hand. Nodding, I ran over to my tool pile. Then I barged my way between Deniz and the step ladder so I could observe the proceedings. Deniz baulked. I held my ground and glowered at him. Evren raised an eyebrow, but said nothing.

Turning to Evren, I smiled ever so sweetly before drawing my archetypal cape about me. Inconspicuously, I pulled out my mental book of spells. Then I took a pen, dipped it in black ink, and began making scratches on the first page.

***

Two hours later, the sun was sinking pink behind the hills, and I was staring at the shade frame. I punched the air. Then I whooped. Because I'd got it. I'd followed the process, and as I'd participated in building the structure from bottom to top, not just my mind but my muscles and cells had absorbed the knowledge too. The secret science of wood structures was a secret no more. I was in in on it.

Turning my back to the shade frame, I faced my land. The dry slope rippled, the stones protruding from the earth like jewels in a breastplate. As evening dropped his veil, I flicked open my eyes and cackled aloud. Finally, I'd done it! I was a hag on a hill. A lone mountain hex. Now I'd sequestered a construction spell. Ha ha! My wand was a hammer. My broomstick a rake. I might have had to scratch it out of the boys, but by hook and by crook I was now empowered.

Standing on the brow of the land, I watched the grass stalks begin to sway. They hissed evocatively as the gloaming coated them. The bushes soon joined the chorus. So did the trees surrounding the land. I sensed the power surging into me, and I cackled a little more. "Oh, we shall make magic now. Lots and lots of construction magic," I said. And right on cue the evening katydids began their eerie trilling.

From the forest I heard a formidable roar. It was rich and rumbling. Dirt Woman's head pushed out from the boughs of a pine tree like that of a loamy Medusa, eyes flashing, dreads coiling. Shaking her fist victoriously at me, she laughed and laughed, before disappearing back into the woods.

The Last Man

I blame Dirt Woman for what happened next. Definitely. Absolutely. It was her. I don't suppose for a minute she'd deny it. She's probably notched the event up on her cave wall, somewhere between a bison and a horse.

We were now sitting squarely in the month of June. The cornflowers had dried up. The broom had shed its buttery petals, and my hill prickled yellow. The good news was that my camp was developing nicely with a functional 'bathroom', and the life-saving tent shade. It was a slatted umbrella of shelter for me, and I would spend my mornings and evenings there happily reading, or daydreaming, on the mat in front of my dome.

The water situation, however, was far from resolved. With every day that passed, it grew more arduous. I cursed the filling of the tanks at the cemetery, the hauling of them into the car, the jolting drive down the road with one hand on the steering wheel, the other stretched behind to prevent the tanks from sliding. Then there was the solicitous hoarding. Each drop was salvaged. I would use a batch of water three times. First, I'd wash food. Then I'd transfer that water to the washing-up bowl. Finally, I'd throw the washing-up water on the three plants I was gamely trying to grow: basil, jasmine, and the sprout of a wild grapevine. It was of course madness to try and grow anything under these conditions. But insanity sometimes has its own wisdom. The jasmine was destined to die, but the basil thrived. And the grapevine eventually grew to be a thick, fruit-laden miracle.

Occasionally, I'd wonder what I was going to do next. But not often. Because something odd was happening to me, and it was a direct result of the land itself. Our planet is a magic mud ball. I'm convinced of it now. We don't even understand half of the power she holds. Now that I was sitting directly on her, touching her, I felt that magic filling me. I was breathing it. Basking in it. A sensation I hadn't really ever known, at least not on this level, was budding on the stem of my experience: I think I'd call it trust. The land had my back. I could feel it. I was safe.

And then I did something stupid. It wasn't the worst mistake I've ever made. But it was a long way from my brightest idea. As I said. I blame the dirt woman. Completely.

"Hey, if you need a hand up there, I can help you." Bartender Lennon pushed a curly wedge of hair behind his ear and cocked his head to one side. He was loitering in Nilay's shop in a black pair of fisherman's pants and not much else. The late afternoon sun was forcing shafts of hot light under the roof, and everyone was perspiring.

"Really?" I said, eyeing him out from a suspicious squint. I was sitting opposite Nilay on a wooden chair, playing with her beads.

"Sure. I'm free all day. And the season hasn't kicked off yet."

"But you sleep all day." I wrinkled my forehead up quizzically and replaced the green stone in its box.

Bartender Lennon grinned and pushed his glasses back on his nose. "Just bang on my tent and shout. I'll get up." He turned and trotted out of the shop, bare feet padding.

Nilay gazed pointedly at me. "Well, I'm sure you could do with a little *help* up there, couldn't you?" She raised her eyebrows a millimetre on the word 'help', before returning her attention to her necklace and nonchalantly jabbing a thread through a bead.

***

Two days later, I was pulling back an orange branch, and shouting at a dilapidated rectangle of plastic.

"Hey, it's midday. Are you free to help me?" The garden was cool despite a zesty sun. A network of pathways crept through the trees, each one ending in a small wooden platform. In the height of the season those platforms would be covered by tents. But for now they were bare.

Bartender Lennon was camped at the far end of the citrus grove. His tent was a canvas survivor from the eighties, one of those rectangular Euro-camp contraptions, sagging, metal poles taped together, and with pale colonies of mildew spreading over the roof. This had been his home for a few years now, except for winter when the Cactus crew returned to Istanbul to spend their days serving bottles of Efes Pilsen in one of Beyoğlu's bars. Later, after the Gezi protests and a government-induced corporate takeover of Taksim Square, the same crowd would move across the Bosphorus to create new alternative haunts in Kadıköy. But this was 2011. Before all progressive hope was flushed down Turkey's ever-failing sewage system.

"Hey, are you awake? Can you help me today, or not?" I rapped on the plastic sheeting again. Then I heard a noise. A sigh. The creak of a mattress spring. The rustle of sheets.

"I'm awake. Just about. Give me five minutes."

"I'm waiting in Nilay's shop," I said, and stepped back into the orange trees.

Fifteen minutes later I was driving up the road. Past the mosque and along the back of the writhing tarmac snake that ferried motor vehicles from the valley to Yapraklı village. Bartender Lennon was beside me rolling a cigarette and looking reasonably well-beaten by the sleep monster. We drove in silence over the brook, through the forest, and into the hamlet. I saw Apo wandering in front of Celal's house. He saw me too and wagged his thick tail before chasing the car all the way to my land.

"So, what do you need help with?" We had drawn to a halt at the base of my slope. The forest was taut, fir trees straining at the ridge trying to move closer.

"I need some more rocks, and I want to finish the terracing you and Celal started under the olive tree. That's going to be my kitchen." Bartender Lennon scratched his beard and nodded. Then he slotted the cigarette into his mouth and opened the car door. The sun fell heavily onto us as we stood at the entrance of the slope.

"No smoking on my land, remember?"

My 'volunteer' yawned in consent.

***

Four hours later, the sun had pulled behind Grandmother Olive leaving the west side of the land pleasantly cool. Bartender Lennon was leaning on a rake admiring his work. And it was a pretty good effort. There were now two separate small terraces instead of one which meant I finally had a space to create a 'proper' kitchen.

"I need to be back at six to get the Cactus bar straight for evening," he said, fumbling in his pants for his tobacco tin.

"Right, let's collect the tools in a pile over there, and then we'll go." I carried a pick and a bucket over to the back of my tent, before grabbing a beach towel hanging on a branch drying, and heading for the car. Lennon was close on my heel.

It was when we were driving back down the curly swirly road – over the bridge, round the bend, across the brook – that she made her appearance. I should have thrown her straight out of the car. I didn't. And that part of the blame rests with me.

Bartender Lennon was sitting in the passenger seat explaining how he'd arrived in the valley. That he'd been thrown out of university in Ankara for protesting about something or other, that his dad was high up in the army and they didn't see eye to eye because he was a communist. It was a tale of Che Guevara flamboyance, and all too common in our secret enclave of Turkey. The Lost City was home to every example of counter culture possible: military service dodgers, scantily-clad feminists (and you probably have to live in Turkey to understand the correlation between those two seemingly oxymoronic concepts), alcoholic artists, hackers, communists, pacifists, environmentalists, animal rights activists, underground wine distillers, pot growers, sex, drugs, and rock and roll à la the sixties. It was something of a wonder the government hadn't shut the place down. Or bombed it with tear gas. Or built a shopping mall on it.

"Why don't you stay for dinner?" Lennon turned from the car window and stared at me a little too hard, a little too long.

"Erm..."

But before I could answer, who should wedge herself between the driver seat and the passenger, but my dirt sister. Her eyes were flashing. She looked like she hadn't eaten for a month. And then it hit me like an avalanche of fossilized rocks where I'd seen her before. Before the land. Before all this reconnecting with nature carnival. No wonder I'd recognised her back in the beginning. Oh dear.

Piss off! Mentally, I batted Dirt Woman with my arm trying to send her to the back seat. I might as well have attempted to change the course of a charging elephant for all the good it did me, because as far as she was concerned, I no longer existed. She was focused on one thing and one thing only. I stared aghast as she began sniffing around Bartender Lennon and licking her lips. I don't think he noticed. But then again...

Gripping the steering wheel, I willed Dirt Woman to leave. I tried to reason with her. No good would come out of a liaison with Bartender Lennon, young and lithe as he might be. It was one colossal waste of energy with no future.

The dirt woman deigned to turn in my direction for a moment. She stared out at me from her raw brown nakedness as though I were some deranged, alien creature. "What is 'fewcha'?" Her mouth struggled with the word as though it were a live insect. "Me know *now*. Me want *now*. Me no care 'fewcha'."

Yes, as if I didn't know. It was then I saw her surreptitiously pull on something. I gulped as I watched a twine made of vines slide into her hands. A net. A man trap. Oh *Lord*!

I'm pretty sure Bartender Lennon saw that net, at least on a Jungian level. And somewhere in the primal earth of his psyche I expect he sharpened his spear, ready to take down the prey. It is after all an ancient game, and one without a winner. Except perhaps for old Gaia, who seems to be the only one who gets what she wants.

***

The next morning when I drove back to my land, I saw the dirt woman on the brow of the hill. She stalked from left to right, shaking her mane like the queen of the jungle. She didn't see me. Stopping for a moment I sensed the invigoration on my skin, the tingle of sexual promise. I wondered if I should simply step out of the way and let her run riot. What would happen if I adopted a bit more of her "me no care fewcha" attitude? Perhaps I should just let go. Leave my destiny to the whims of instinct and fate.

And then I spied them, beyond the dirt woman. Grandmother Olive and her two smaller olive sisters. Light shimmered wistfully over the ridges that had settled into their bark, so that they formed a thicket of reflection. I heard the ripple of doom somewhere far away. The steady inching forward of a cold, dark tide. Fewcha. Care about it or not, it would still arrive.

Ancestral Powers

Summer was coming. Evenings had become warm seas of crickets and jasmine. The days were by and large considered to be too long.

"Ooh, I hate it!" said Dudu. "It's as if the sun never goes down."

She had a point. The sun was greedy in the summer months. It monopolised the sky from five am until nine pm. But I wasn't complaining, because the sun had long since become my eyes.

I still had no mains electricity, and to be honest I didn't much care any more. In what might be the most abrupt switch of personality ever to hit a psychologist's desk, I had come to love the clean silence of a powerless environment, and the brightness of the stars. Electricity always seems to beget noise, doesn't it? Drills, saws, televisions, loud speakers, terrible music, blenders, vacuum cleaners, lawn mowers. But there was something else. An added bonus. Living without electricity had forged this direct channel to the lair of my dirt woman. It was through a plugless, bulbless, butt-in-dirt survivalism that I connected with her properly. With the real. The untamed.

I would often close my eyes and see Dirt Woman squatting at the entrance of her cave, sniffing the air, senses as sharp as a knife edge. As I stared at her through the telescope of time, I saw her power. She had access to special abilities, to the instinctive knowledge of our ancestors. And that knowledge was within me too, rattling about in a dusty, cobweb-draped spiral of my DNA. Now I understood. The conveniences of the modern world have suppressed our ancient inheritance. It's a muscle we've forgotten how to use. We have been tricked by urbanity and technology into flaccid passivity. Into dependence. Into a deformed shadow of what we humans really are.

Since first meeting the dirt woman I had gone through a type of metamorphosis. My strength and agility had transformed. Here I was at almost forty years old able to complete physical tasks I couldn't have managed even in my twenties. And so quickly! It staggered me how fast my body had adapted.

My relationship to time and space had also changed. I was starting to sense the movement of hours without a clock, and directions without a map. The sun was no longer simply a distant solarium or day-trip enabler. It was my compass, my light, my clock, and my guide. It became so obvious how and why the ancients had worshipped this beautiful golden orb. I was worshipping it! And the moon. And the stars.

Another evolution I was going through was sensitivity. Noises, smells, the movement of light and colour, all were now things I was developing a keen awareness of. Because all signified something. Eventually I would be able to tell the time just by seeing how the light was falling, and the colour of the grass or trees.

Later I would learn, we humans actually come wired with an ocular clock, and can sense exactly how much daylight is left by the colour tone of our surroundings. Humans have two types of photoreceptors in the retina, rods and cones, which contribute to our visual perception in different ways. The rod system is extremely sensitive to light but has low spatial resolution, while the cone system has high spatial resolution and allows us to see colour, but is relatively insensitive to light. Thus in daylight it is the cones that primarily contribute to our seeing (colour and depth), while at night the rods take over. At twilight, something called Mesopic vision occurs[6]. At this time both rods and cones contribute to our visual perception, and as the light wanes, the cone contribution reduces. Thus we instinctively know from the amount of colour we see where we are in the day. Or we *should* know. For artificial light and an obsession with clocks has now made us somewhat blind.

Yet amazing as it was, this sensory awareness wasn't the most profound shift I experienced. For me, the most

6   **"Neuroscience 2"**, Purves D, Augustine GJ, Fitzpatrick D, et al.' editors. Sunderland (MA):Sinauer Associates; 2001

significant impact of the land was on my mood. For reasons that were illogical according to modernity, despite lacking basic amenities like running water and a house, I was wandering around each day holding a deep and pervading sense of fulfilment. I was happy. Simply happy. It was a different type of joy to any I'd really known before. It wasn't the brief hit of gratification, nor the rush of acquisition. It seemed to be more of an aura that surrounded me. And it cost nothing.

Most days I'd wander the length of the forest edge. And when I did I'd peer inside. Dry pine needles and Mediterranean oak leaves formed a crunchy carpet, the tree boughs curled untamed, birds trilled, insects buzzed, and the nooks rustled with small mammals and reptiles. Sometimes I'd see Dirt Woman there gazing at a dragonfly or gnawing a carob. She possessed none of the restless drive of her descendants. There were no plans and schemes darting across her face. Her world was one of natural cues. She responded to the moment. And the moment responded to her in return.

"How do you decide what to do?" I asked one day. "I mean don't you get bored without a project?"

Dirt Woman blinked at me. She was squatting under a carob tree, chewing on a stick and studying a beetle that was scurrying over her arm.

"Bored? What is this bored? I don't know bored."

"It's...it's..." I stopped to think. What did it really mean to be bored? And it was a pertinent question because boredom had always been a type of hell for me. I paused to consider what it was about boredom that I found so intolerable. I sat next to the Dirt Woman for a moment, closed my eyes, and found the sensation of tedium.

"It's when you don't have anything interesting or exciting to do, and a terrible feeling arises."

"What feeling?"

I pulled out the feeling from my emotional memory banks. A stultifying heaviness pressed on my sternum, and I felt sick.

"It's like suffocating. Or being strangled. Like you can't breathe," I put both hands round my throat and acted being throttled.

Dirt Woman stared at me, eyes fixed on my throat in scrutiny.

"So problem is this feeling. Like you no free. Like somebody press you. But nobody press you, so why you feel like this?"

It was a good question.

"I tell you why," she said. "Because you no feel joined with all of us. You lose your root. With no root you lose your power and you feel small and in cage."

"I don't know really. But if I was living like you, I'd feel I should be doing something more useful."

"What you think more 'useful'?" Dirt Woman let the beetle crawl onto her index finger. She brought the brown digit in front of her nose and continued to watch the black insect skipping over her skin.

Yes, what *did* I think was more useful? Working a job that made some psychopath richer so that he could destroy more of the planet? Earning money to spend it on something that obviously didn't really satisfy my deeper desires? Making a wash rack? Making myself more comfortable so that I could then sit around and feel bored?

"You know what? I don't know what's more useful really. I've been brainwashed by a bunch of puritans. It's like there's a brutal charioteer in my head, whipping me on, never letting me sit and be." I stood briefly and pretended to ferociously whip the air in front of me to convey the idea to my muddy friend.

And this was where things turned interesting. I soon realised my earthy ancestor was far cleverer than I was giving her credit for. Dirt Woman gently placed her finger on the leaf mulch, and the beetle crawled quickly off into the dry leaves. Then she stood up, put her hand on my shoulder, and stared into my eyes. Again I saw the fires burning in the back of them. And something else. Something I'd sensed but not quite conceptualised.

Power. Raw, unstoppable power. It was so profound, so unfathomable, I drew in a sharp breath.

"You must kill this bad man in your head," Dirt Woman said without a soupçon of a flinch. Bending down, she picked up a long stick. Next she focused on the space I'd been whipping a minute earlier. Silently, she drew her arm behind her, and then snapped it forward. The stick drove into the earth, skewering my fantasy charioteer into the humus like a şiş kebab. Dirt Woman spun back to me. "When you hear this bad man, you must kill him. Quick! Don't let him speak. He your enemy."

I blinked at the stick upended in the ground and scratched my temple. Good *Lord*!

"Don't you think it's a bit drastic? I mean, I don't really believe in killing."

Dirt Woman now placed both her hands on my shoulders. "If you no believe killing, why you let bad man in your head kill *you*? I say you, this...this..." Here, she pulled an arm back and made a mouth out of her hand. Then she opened and closed it like a glove puppet while emitting a number of tyrannical sounding noises.

"Voice?"

"This voice...It no living thing. It poison and try to kill you. It suck your power and happy feeling. Don't feel sorry for poison. Just kill it."

I'll be honest here. While half of me was somewhat appalled, the other half of me, the half of me that is wolf not bunny rabbit, couldn't wait. Dirt Woman was right. There were far too many bleating, whining, cajoling voices in my head, voices that I'd adopted from childhood no doubt, voices that had seeped from one generation to another, infecting each new mind with their worthless attachment to drudge and enslavement. I screwed up my fist and punched my mud sister lightly on the shoulder. She punched me back harder and guffawed so loudly a tree full of birds twittered into the sky.

Inhaling the hot, resiny air, I felt my feet on the Earth drawing in the power of the planet. It was as though I had roots sinking into the soil, connecting me to the source of it all. Yeees. Perhaps Dirt Woman was right. Perhaps it was time for a bit of a cull.

But what happens when we fight back against our conditioning? Is there a price to pay?

***

It was the next morning, and I sensed the darkness easing back from the tent. Blinking, I caught sight of the lights of Adrasan extinguishing as the silver of dawn slunk into the bay. The birds were chirping madly in the forest next door, sometimes flitting past the tent opening. Yawning, I stretched an arm out of my sleeping bag. And then the sun stalked onto the catwalk of the sky wearing a robe of shocking pink. The mountain ridges sat bolt upright, the roof of the valley glowed, and the forests sparkled their applause.

Dirt Woman sniffed the air, leapt on all fours, and let rip a caterwaul. This was morning. And she was going to devour it. I held her inside my mind and body. Today we were on a rock-shifting mission. I was going to need her. But not only her. As I would learn, I was going to need something else too. Something that would give me a power I had never previously known. This ordinary-appearing rock task was going to be a major turning point. I'd even say the construction of my future earthbag house rested upon the lesson I was about to learn. Namely, that there is far more than physical strength involved in making things happen.

"Me like rocks. Me make good wall. You see." My dirt woman stomped her feet and whooped.

"Okay. Let's do this then." I knew full well it was going to be more than just a case of 'you see'. I adjusted my cap, pulled on my work gloves, and grabbed the pick. Continuing the semicircle Celal had started, I dug a small trench to sit the rocks in. This task alone would have taken me an entire morning two months ago. Bit by bit, I was learning to channel Dirt Woman's strength.

Finding three meaty rocks, I lifted them and slotted them into place, relishing the sensation of my biceps expanding and contracting. Within half an hour the wall was complete and looking rather professional, if I may say so.

I stood up and patted Dirt Woman on the back. She grinned. It was a frightening hyena's snarl of a smile, but never mind. The trouble was, the woman from the clay wasn't content with simply finishing the wall. I learned over time she was never content until she had me on my back wheezing in exhaustion. There was a rock stuck in the middle of the semicircle I'd finished. It poked out of the earth like a wisdom tooth needing extraction, rucking the flat surface of the semicircle which I had planned to turn into a shaded sitting area.

"Alright, let's get that thing out," I said. "And use it as a seat."

Dirt Woman nodded. "I move rock, you see. Woo hoo!"

Studying the rock a little closer, I saw it was submerged deeply in the earth. I grabbed the pick, and dug as much soil away from the base of it as I could. Then I laid my hands around it, leaned back, and yanked. There was much grunting. I heaved and sweated and gurned. The rock stayed put.

"Rock very heavy. Me find different rock," huffed the dirt woman.

"No, we need *this* rock. It's enchanting, with a perfect flat surface, and will make an amazing seat. That is the rock we want," I said. But whilst I wanted it, I could see just how big it was, and how well-wedged in the ground.

Walking around the boulder, I kicked it with my boot. It didn't so much as shudder. Then I knelt and slid my hand around the base, trying to assess how deeply embedded it was. Finally, I sat down on the rock itself, my facial muscles drooping like the leaves of my basil plant under the midday sun. *It's too big. I can't get it out. I don't even know if Celal will manage it. I'm just not strong enough*. The thoughts slid out from various gutters in my mind like cognitive vermin, and a hollow sinking feeling made itself known in my chest. *I'm never going to be able to do this, it's impossible*. Slowly my drive began to seep away. I felt my back slump.

Ah, the mind. How powerful it is, and how poorly we understand it. One thought can change your entire psychological state. And that in turn transforms the physiological. It is the deciding factor in whether you will or won't make something happen.

I looked up to see Dirt Woman standing a few feet away, arms folded over her chest, scrutinizing me. "Why you tired now? What happen?"

"We can't do it," I shrugged.

"Who say we can't do it?"

"I don't know. It just seems stuck. It will take hours."

"I tell you who say we can't do it. It is the poison. Head poison."

Jolting my chin up, I gaped at my dirt friend, because by Jove, she was right! I jumped to my feet suddenly remembering about the charioteer, and the negative voices in my head, and how Dirt Woman had told me to slay them. Hmph! I opened and closed my fists. I was awake at last. Yet this time I realised, the poisoned voice in my head wasn't the charioteer. It was different. Who was this snide, energy-sucking weasel telling me I couldn't do something? Telling me that it was impossible? How did this mental voice *know* it was impossible? Why was I believing it? Abruptly, such an outrage exploded within me, I was surprised by it.

"Fuck this! This is bullshit!" I shouted. And in my mind's eye I saw a hundred dark winged bats flurry into holes. "Don't tell *me* I can't do this!"

Somewhere a shadow rose, and I wondered briefly if there would be some kind of retribution for killing off a personal demon. But something else inside me, something instinctive, raw, and true was now running over the plains of my mind, spear in hand. I watched enthralled as Dirt Woman cantered on to the scene, pulling her arm back like a javelin thrower. She lunged and drove the spike straight into my shadow, piercing it. It crumpled in a deflated heap between us.

In a flash, my physiology changed. Vitality rolled into me in waves. I expanded. I had energy. And I knew I was going to get that damn rock out. I was sure. The only question now was *how*?

Now that I was no longer feeling hopeless and beaten, my mind opened itself to solutions and to the place I was in. The land responded. The rocks, trees, and grasses grew distinct edges. They stood out as though craning their necks to see me. Colours became clearer. Sounds were sharper. And then I smelt Grandmother Olive only a few metres from where I was standing.

Turning quickly around, I stared at her. The sun was now behind her, and her branches looked like they were lobbing sunbeams out into the land and sky. Inhaling deeper, I savoured her aroma. And then of course the ideas began to rain down upon me.

"If a thought can change a mood, dear, if it can change the biochemistry of a human body, what else can it change?"

I closed my eyes and sensed the truth of this. Three minutes prior I had been sitting on a rock, doing nothing, feeling hopeless and with no energy. Now I was standing up, excited, and buzzing with resolve. The only thing that had caused that change were my thoughts.

"Your world doesn't end at your fingertips. It's all moving in sync. Me, you, the ground, the air, the rock. We are all affecting each other. So see the rock Earth-child, and use your mind to *imagine* it is out. Don't waver. Don't doubt it. See it, feel it, and believe it. Then *act*!"

Pulling my gaze from the tree, I gawped at the rock. It was a superb boulder, as white and flat as marble. Shrugging, I called on Dirt Woman again. Well, there wasn't much to lose from trying, was there? I inhaled and exhaled deeply, focused my eyes on the rock, and then lunged.

A good few minutes of pulling ensued. Urgh! Agh! Argh! Oof! The rock wobbled ever so slightly. I heaved more. Shouted more. But in the end I let go, pinging back as if on elastic. This beast of limestone was still stuck. And I had depleted my energy reserves. I sat on the earth and sighed. My ancient sister bowed her head.

"Me rest a minute," she wheezed.

We sat there for a minute, lungs heaving. But almost immediately a voice flicked over from behind us.

"Three. Everything works in threes. Three is the magic number. You've only tried twice. You must always attempt a task three times."

I was impatient now. The rock was mine. Grabbing the dirt woman by the arm, I walked over to it. "Okay. Pay attention. The rock is coming out. I can feel it moving. I can see it yanked out of its socket. It's a beautiful seat, right there." I pointed at a space in the semicircle. Dirt Woman began to breathe in and out of her nostrils noisily.

"Do you see the rock pulled out?" I asked. She nodded.

Small bubbles of excitement started to pop inside me. The atmosphere tightened, as though the air was now Perspex.

"One. Two. *Three...*"

I leaned into the rock. Boom! It was as if my mind had penetrated its skin and began pulling it from within. Sheer willpower drove through me and into the boulder. I felt it budge. Gritting my teeth, my abdomen contracted into a hunk of steel. I refused to let it fall back. It was coming. It was shifting. Good grief! It was...out!

I collapsed on the ground both startled and exhausted in equal measure. Dirt Woman immediately pounced on top of the rock, stretched out her arms, and roared.

Oh, how well I remember this moment. This was *it*. In an instant, my world had grown larger, and I realised I might be able to do far more than I had previously thought, maybe even *anything*. The rock caper had galvanised something inside me and squeezed it into seam of iron ore. Suddenly the doubt was gone, and in its place flourished a new self-belief, or was it life-belief?

Ultimately, it was the yanking of that rock that led me to trust I could make things happen. All kinds of things. Within five months, despite having not known how to bang a nail in, I'd be building my very own house! Later I would also build websites (notwithstanding the fact I was so technologically inept at that time I couldn't even use internet banking). And most importantly of all for my soul, I'd be writing and publishing the books I'd dreamed of. Until that moment so many of these dreams had been lumbering about inside me, but had been unable to crawl out from their warrens to bounce and breathe in the light. They were trapped by the head poison and a lack of self-belief.

Panting a little, I went to sit under Grandmother Olive. Now that the rock task was complete, my muscle-clad dirt pal loped off into the trees of my deep psyche again. I wondered briefly what she would do for the rest of the day. Talk with a squirrel? Sleep in the carob tree?

Settling into the hammock, I decided to talk with my old olive tree in earnest about all that had happened. The hammock purred gently as the rope tightened and relaxed. I stared into the divaricating world of leaves and twigs that was Grandmother Olive. Each branch was a fork in the road, leading to another fork, and another. The tree was a living, growing flowchart.

I sighed, and then spoke. "Look, on the one hand this slaying of mental negativity feels great. I mean it's as liberating as hell! But what if some of the voices in my head are trying to protect me? Do you think Dirt Woman is right that this is all head poison and that these voices are all enemies to be eradicated?"

"Ah, it's so simple, my dear." The words bubbled through me as effortlessly as water in a brook.

"Is it?"

"Yes! If the voice uplifts you, fills you with well-being, makes you feel loved and cherished and supported, if it inspires you and generates happiness or peace within you, if it sounds like your friend, then it *is* your friend."

"And if it doesn't?"

The wind gently pushed the branches to and fro. I heard the familiar patter of dried-up olives hitting the ground around me.

"If it makes you feel guilt, shame, worthlessness, hopelessness or fear, it is a predator thought."

"Predator thought? What do you mean? Where do they come from then, these predator thoughts? Aren't they mine?"

"Your mind is powerful. It can make miracles or it can destroy you. And many have used thought to control people over the centuries, via media of all kinds, education, conditioning. But mostly people are simply believing their own conditioning and regurgitating it to others, not understanding what they are doing. Thus humans become filled with fear and worry, most of which isn't really theirs."

"I always thought they were *my* thoughts. But they're not, are they? That's a pretty disturbing realisation. It's like an invasion!"

"It matters little. No conditioning, no mental voice or personal demon is a match for the awakened human spirit. As you see."

I think this was the single most important thing I learned up on Mud Mountain. All power is in truth power over the mind. If you weed out the negative voices, get your thoughts in line, and point them in the right direction, everything else follows suit. And on the odd occasion it doesn't?

Ah well, I've come to trust life is usually doing me a favour. That someone somewhere in my soul knows more than I do.

Three Fugitives

"Here you go, my girl." Dudu thrust a metal plate spilling over with triangles of watermelon onto the table in front of me. Not even bothering with the fork she had placed beside it, I grabbed a wedge and crammed it into my mouth. The sweet juice ran down my chin. I didn't care. It was delicious.

"Ay, nowt like a home-grown melon is there?" Celal was sitting at the other end of the plastic table. He picked up a teaspoon and began shovelling sugar into his tea glass. I lost count after three spoonfuls.

We were sitting in front of Dudu's house under a large shade she'd created out of a grapevine. The vine was expansive and abounding. Thick stems crisscrossed over a wire frame from which bundles and bundles of leaves pushed out. I gawped up at the living canopy longingly. "Oh, I wonder how long it will take for *my* grapevine to grow," I asked, reaching for another slice of pink paradise.

Dudu plonked herself onto the spare plastic chair, and shuffled there for a minute, her şalwars ballooning about her hips. "Which grapevine?" Her feet dangled a good few inches from the ground, and she swung them as she spoke. She really was very short, even by Anatolian standards.

"There's bit of an old grape, someone musta chucked a seed down there once, and it grew. Not much though. Don't even reach yer knee." Celal sucked at the rim of his tea glass disdainfully, quickly draining the glass.

"Ah, it's a trick grape. Nothing will come of *that*," said Dudu, shaking her head. She pushed some hair back under her headscarf and huffed.

"Trick grape? What's a trick grape?" I peered up from my melon wedge.

Celal pushed his tea glass in Dudu's direction for a refill. "'S not proper," he said. "Won't grow. It'll just give piddly old grapes, and they'll be sour little buggers too."

"Why don't you get yourself a real grape?" Dudu barked.

"Because I want to make *that* one grow. It was already there on the land."

"But you don't have water." My little old neighbour poured more tea from her two-tiered pot, first the rich red brew, then a steaming top-up with water.

"I'm throwing my washing-up water on it at the moment. It might survive."

Both Dudu and Celal raised their eyebrows and tutted. Then they sighed. Finally, they folded their arms and shook their heads.

"'S not gonna work."

I pushed a third triangle of watermelon into my mouth and sucked on it, ignoring the pair of them. The vine was a resident of my land, so I was going to care for it. Since the ant episode everything in my land felt part of a team. I was sure that grapevine would grow, because I was going to love it into existence.

Looking up, I saw Dudu pull a plate onto her lap. It was filled with cracked wheat. Deftly, her experienced hands began to sort the bulgur. As usual, I gaped in amazement, because there was nothing this woman couldn't make. She was pretty much self-sufficient. She pressed her own olive oil and pomegranate molasses; she grew all her own fruit, vegetables and herbs. She made her own tomato puree and carob molasses. Her flat breads were piled up in her kitchen like a tower of enormous poppadoms, and there were endless pickles and olives and dried fruits too. She was nearly seventy, owned a hectare of land filled with trees and produce, and managed it almost single-handedly except for the summer tree-watering when family would sometimes pop up for the weekend. She thought this was all quite typical, but for me it was an incredible life. She was my survivalist hero.

"Ahem." It was Celal who coughed. His shoulders jerked upwards. The little man began to squirm on his stool, and the lines around his eyes started to twitch. It looked as though he had something of personal importance to expound. Finally, he rested his tea glass on the plastic table, and made the subject of his twitching known.

"I'm gonna move into my hut next summer. I've decided," he spat the sentence out onto the table, leaving it to glisten in front of us.

I blinked. Leaning back on my chair, I peered past Dudu's house, and from there I could just about see Celal's hut. The small wooden shack perched uncomfortably on the hillside, and depending on your point of view it was either a crime of engineering or a miracle of amateur carpentry. Celal had built it himself, much of it out of recycled materials. He'd gathered the timber and wooden cladding from another dismantled shed, the tiles were second-hand, and the windows and doors were from scrapyards. It was actually rather funky in my opinion. But to *live* in it?

"Do you think it's safe?" I said. "I mean, it won't fall down on you, will it?" I glanced over at the wonky wooden stilts it was squatting upon. It resembled some sort of spindly-legged creature, and a drunk one at that.

"Bin fine for two winters," Celal sniffed and downed his second glass of tea. Dudu remained tactfully diffident. She stood up, tucked her headscarf in once again, and poured Celal and me yet another glass of tea. Eventually, she broke the silence.

"Yes, it will be just fine. You can keep all your food in my fridge, can't you? And fill up your water here too if you need to."

"Gonna get water from the borough," Celal said.

"Yes, but until then..."

"But why?" I blurted. "You have a decent house in the village. Why do you want to live up here?"

"Me kids are in my house. You know, they're a young couple. I mean we have two kitchens and the like, but I wanna sit in me own house, on me own land, with me own trees. Everyone needs their space."

And isn't *that* the truth?

Looking at Dudu and Celal in turn, I chuckled. We were a rum lot, hugging the outskirts of Yaprakli village like three self-sufficient fugitives. Celal in his hut with Apo the dog, Dudu in her house churning out a never-ending stream of natural produce, and me, the crazy English woman in the tent. Lord knows why I was surprised at Celal's decision when I was at least ten steps closer to lunacy than he was.

This need for a space of one's own is so primal. It is such a basic yearning. A garden, a shelter, and sovereignty over your own territory. As a woman, I knew why I was going to the limits for it. In a world where the game plan has mostly been designed by men for men, I wanted a space to be free, a place where I could have room just to see who I really was, and what I was capable of. I wanted to dress how I felt like, be ugly or pretty and have it not matter, to expand in my personal power. But what I wanted most of all was to create my own world. One that adhered to *my* values.

And perhaps this was why I was surprised at Celal. I understood Dudu. I understood myself. Both Dudu and I were survivors from The Man's World in our different ways. But I hadn't considered that some men were in cages too. To be a sensitive, caring man, to be a man who hears the animals and plants, a man with a heart in a boarish, brutally systematic, and mostly moronic culture, is hard.

"Yes, it's great to be alone on your own land, Celal. You can do exactly what you want!" I felt my grin stretching so wide it made my cheeks smart.

"Aye. I can see it is." Celal chuckled. Apo raised his fluffy dog head and nuzzled the brown twig of his owner's leg.

As I sat with my two neighbours, such a tenderness rose inside me. We differed from each other in so many ways: in age, gender, and ethnicity. Yet here was this bond. And it gleamed and shone like a golden thread, winding around our love of our gardens, our independence, and our space. This is the truth of being human. The powers that be can segregate us and label us as much as they want, but in essence all people, male and female, black, brown and white, Eastern and Western, right-wing and left-wing, come wired with the same underlying drives: to be free to express themselves, to love and be loved, and to grow.

Without warning, Dudu piped up, throwing something of a maladroit rolling pin into the works. "But why don't you get married, Kerry?" she said abruptly. "You are still young!" She folded her hands under her bosom, her face folding in confusion.

"Would you get married again, Dudu?" I shot back feeling my nostrils widen in impatience. The sun forced its way through the small holes in the grapevine burning various parts of my open skin.

"*Allah Allah!* Noooo. I've done my stint," Dudu said. Her lips were shaped as though she were whistling.

"So if *you* wouldn't do it, why do you wish such a fate on me?"

"Ooh, I'm an old bat! You're young! You still look nice. You can find a man before it's too late."

"Too late for *what*? I'm happy. I'm free. I don't have to put up with anyone else's bad behaviour or use up my valuable energy cooking and cleaning and doing things I hate. If you want to get married, you do it. Me? I've looked in that box and it's empty. I'm almost forty, and I'm not wasting a minute more."

Yes. There is much romanticism regarding Eastern cultures by moderns hungering for community and respite from the hyper-individualism of the West. Having lived in the heart of the Anatolia for twenty years, I can tell you. The shape of The System may change, but it's all pretty much the same story in the end. Ultimately, whichever culture you're in, if you don't squash yourself within the confines of its narrow dictates, you are an outcast. In the West social norms circumnavigate the purchase of houses and cars, the climbing of some poxy career ladder, and getting a 'hot' partner to brag about. In rural Anatolia you need to get married, have children, and tiptoe past a minefield of activities considered shameful.

"So you're going to live alone *forever*?" Dudu's eyes bulged a little.

"There are things I want to create before I die. I'm desperate to write and paint and make things. I can't do those things when I'm with someone else. The energy just dies in me."

"Are you writing books?" My small neighbour's face became animated, eyebrows rising in anticipation.

"Well..." I shifted on my chair and began to stare at the dirt. "I'm trying to write one."

There were oohs and ahhs from both Celal and Dudu.

"That's why I want to be up here and be peaceful. All alone. Quiet." Remaining seated, I shunted my plastic chair sideways into a new patch of shade, before sitting back and wiping a little sweat from the sides of my nose with my fingers. "I just don't understand why you keep on about being married, Dudu. Are *you* unhappy alone?"

"No. If I feel lonely I just walk into the village and visit someone," she said. Then she pushed her lips out thoughtfully. "I suppose getting married is just what we all do, isn't it? It's just the way it is."

Above and around us, Dudu's grapevine stirred, stalks straining like woody ears. The sun shifted ever so slightly, and the mottled patterns the leaves' shadows created on the ground changed. A new fretwork of shade moved over the clean white table. Sunlight found fresh territory on our heads. All three of us sat quiet, feeling the hot breath of the air, and hearing the regular strum of the crickets.

Someone New

The valley had tipped into the month of July. It was a headlong tumble from here into steam and sweat and heat rash. The sun strode over the sky, confident, full-bodied, knowing the next two months were his and his alone.

On my camp, the brunt of the survival structures were complete. I'd just completed my third attempt at a kitchen area. I'd moved it from the side of my tent to under Grandmother Olive. Laying a plank over Celal's wall, I created a shelf. I'd acquired yet another old table from Nilay and Evren, and used it as a worktop. I'd also found a wooden chest of drawers fit for the dumpster, painted it and positioned the gas cylinder on it. This was my 'hob'. My frying pan and a few utensils hung from the branches of a scrawny wild oak. It was a great kitchen, if I say so myself, and I'd still be using it when the floods of winter came.

And then someone new appeared in my world. Well, he was thrust into it really, because the truth was I had no interest in getting to know another person. But life is curious. Some things are just meant to be, no matter how hard you try to avoid them.

***

"I don't want to meet anyone. I told you, I'm antisocial," I grumbled, stabbing a cube of feta. Lennon and I were sitting in Café Cactus having breakfast.

Lennon sipped on his tea, and reached for a boiled egg. "You'll like these two, I tell you. Oof, just come and say hello, alright?" The garden was filling up now. One by one, yawning bed-haired people staggered from the bathroom to the bar to collect their eggs, olives, and tea. Lennon picked up his plate and stood up. "Don't disappear!"

I scowled at him, with every intention of doing just that. "I want to go home. To my land. I just want to sit up there in nature."

"You always want to be up there on your land. Bloody nature! It's everywhere!" He shook his shaggy head and padded into the bar.

As the crickets cranked up their buzzing and the sun forged higher, I felt the water level rising inside me. Chilly. Murky. Comfortless. I began to wonder as I sat there just why talking with humans was so much less fulfilling than whispering with a tree. On the horizon of my emotions I saw a dark wave. It rolled and lurched toward me in nauseating inevitability. I stood up and walked out of the garden.

But I was too late.

My car was parked under an immense pine tree just in front of the dry riverbed. Next to it was a white Fiat Alba, a hire car. A small Indian-looking man and a young blonde woman were chatting behind it.

"This is Adnan," Lennon called out, loping over from the garden. "Adnan, this is Kerry."

Groaning, I mentally turned the ignition of my social cyborg. Was it me, or did I catch this Adnan chap doing the same? We both looked each other up and down with the measured judiciousness typical of long-term foreigners who don't consider themselves foreign. Adnan cocked his head to one side.

"Hey there!" He stretched his hand out, and I shook it apathetically as I noted the North-American accent.

"Adnan's an odd name for an American." I squinted at him. As far as I knew it was a Turkish name. I hoped he wasn't one of those people that had adopted a fake local name to fit in or something.

"I'm Canadian, but born in Pakistan. It's a Pakistani name too, and in Canada everyone pronounces it Adnarn."

I blinked at the unfamiliarity of the drawn-out vowels. Adnan chuckled. "And *this*," he withdrew his hand and opened his palm toward the woman, "is my girlfriend, Annika."

"Hallo!" Annika pumped my hand enthusiastically, and I clocked the German accent. She was a bookish blonde in her twenties. Adnan was older. Maybe in his thirties.

Casting an eye at my car, I cut to the chase. "So, what are you doing here?"

Adnan inflated ever so slightly. "I'm a journalist, escaping from Istanbul. I'm renting a house up there." He pointed to the steeply rising hills behind us. "Really quiet. No one around. Just a creepy cemetery. I don't think it's haunted but hey..." He chortled and smoothed his ebony fringe down.

Something clanked in one of the back rooms of my mind. Cemetery? No. It *couldn't* be mine. My area was only inhabited by pomegranate farmers and greenhouses of aubergines. All foreigners remained in the folds of the Lost City where they could prance about in bikinis and lounge on platforms nuzzling bottles of cold beer. I shrugged off the coincidence.

***

It was a strikingly-hot summer morning a week or so later, and much to my bewilderment, I was wandering onto Adnan's balcony. I gaped incredulously as I trotted up the steps. An enormous almond tree shaded the small terrace. It was dripping with green furry pockets. The house was perched between two beautiful traditional stone huts, more recently used as barns. It was idyllic. But that wasn't the reason for my surprise.

"You're my neighbour!" I blurted.

"Huh?"

"You're my frigging neighbour!"

"I don't have a neighbour as far as I know," said Adnan sliding a plate onto the small table that sat in the centre of the pretty veranda. The dish was filled with feta cubes and oregano, with olive oil drizzled over. I shunted this cheese platter next to the small bowls of honey, jam, and butter already laid out.

"Well, I'm pretty sure I'm the nearest other human to your house."

"No. That is very *strange!*" Annika appeared, and quickly moved the feta plate and squeezed a saucer of cut tomatoes next to it, before disappearing back into the house from which a number of sizzlings and spittings emanated.

Why I had ended up going to breakfast at Adnan's is beyond me. He had invited both me and Lennon the day we met in the Lost City. And for some reason, I had accepted the invitation. Maybe it was because he was a writer, and I dreamed of being one. Perhaps it was because he'd travelled overland through Pakistan as I had, and I had never met anyone else who had braved the trip. Whatever it was, the stars must have aligned fortuitously that day, because looking back on it, it was one of the most serendipitous social decisions I'd ever make. Whether Adnan would think the same way, I wouldn't care to say. If he had known we'd soon all be knee-deep in dirt, building an earthbag house, would he have run for cover? Probably not. He liked adventure. He also liked cooking, which was excellent news for me.

None of this, however, assisted me with my current challenge: fitting a breakfast for what appeared to be a dozen people onto a table designed for two. I began shifting the tea glasses to make room for the bread basket. Annika appeared again with two bowls of olives, one black, one green, and immediately snuck them into the carefully-created gap.

"What do you write about?" I shouted toward the kitchen, holding the bread basket lamely and wondering what to do with it.

Adnan walked out onto the balcony with a sizzling pan. "Wars. Middle Eastern politics. I was in Iraq and Afghanistan, that's where I met Annika."

"I'm an anthropologist," Annika said, face scintillating with all the optimism of the young and in love. She was fresh and open. Inwardly I groaned. Because the trouble with age and experience, and being a witch, is that you know exactly how that optimism ends.

"Come on, guys! Make a space for the eggs!" Adnan pushed the egg pan closer. The breakfast table tessellation game had reached level nine. I scanned the clutter of food-filled crockery, adding together the empty areas between the plates in my mind in search of a spare frying-pan of space. "Oh no! Where the hell are we going to put *those*?"

Annika snickered and picked up her plate. "You always make so much, Adnan!"

"Guests should never go hungry!" My new journo neighbour beamed. "Hey there, come and eat, brother." He called over the rail of the balcony to Lennon who was sitting by the fire-pit stabbing at the cold ash with a snapped-off almond twig.

Lennon huffed, stood up, and trudged toward the table. His beard covered most of his mouth; nevertheless, it was obvious the corners were drooping. I didn't know what he was miserable about, but I immediately felt a slump. Hopelessness wafted over the waves of my soul like murky sea mist. It was as if my life energy was slowly but surely being drained out of my heart. As I sat there on Adnan's balcony watching the beautiful almond tree fluttering gently in the sun, it suddenly dawned on me. This was how I always felt in relationships: Unfulfilled. Disappointed. Tired.

I blinked. Then I raised my Turkish tulip glass and took a sip of tea. Why was I still doing this? Why was I pinning hopes of happiness on something so obviously hopeless?

While I sat at the table for two eating a breakfast for twelve, I pondered. Who did I actually know in a relationship that I envied? That I would swap places with? The tight clusters of almonds bobbed up and down on Adnan's tree, as all the couples I'd met began to flash up in my mind's eye. The clipped wings. The dependency. The domestic smallness both parties had to maintain not to rock the boat. The permissions asked.

The eggshells walked on. And I knew I couldn't do it. Because I was a witch of the dirt. Not a wife. Not a mother. mother. Not a people-pleaser nor family-holder-togetherer. I wanted to break all the rules, grate them into chips and throw them in my composting toilet. I wanted to be bossy and big, flamboyant and ferocious, antisocial and uncouth. I wanted to cackle and play with scorpions. And fuck it. I was almost forty. So if I didn't wake up and live my truth now, when would I?

In a couple of days I drove down to the valley and unpinned myself from Lennon. It wasn't anyone's fault. It was simply without *fewcha*, or present, or meaning. On the way back, I wended my way along the small village road through the forest. As I left the tarmac, and drove onto the dirt track to my home, I felt both sorrow and relief in equal measure. Because I could sense just how deep the rut of conditioning to partner-up and form a family. And how unnervingly boundless life looked without it.

The car swerved this way and that, churning up dust like a genie. My land slid into view. Feeling my old Fiat taking the bumps in her stride, I held my breath, wondering what life would be like now that I had binned the lauded aim of the relationship as well.

Potions

It was seven o'clock, and the inside of my tent was so infernally hot, I could barely breathe. The month of August was sitting squarely upon us now. I gave lolling in bed my best shot, but when my toes and fingertips started sweating I knew I had to quit. Thus, I unzipped the door and staggered out into the day.

Forlornly I surveyed my world. It had become a slope of yellow expiration. The top terrace of the land, where my tent was pitched, was a Sahara of baked soil and scorched grass stalks. Cracks zigzagged through the waterless earth. And where there were no cracks, there was dust.

Water. I so needed water! And I groaned at the thought of filling up my containers yet again. One hundred metres below me, the canal gleamed tantalizingly. It was a limpid vein pulsing along the dry leg of the road. Perhaps I should try and talk to whichever officious little local patrolled the gates of the channel. Perhaps I should purchase a pump. Every day that passed the value of water increased in my mind. I had never realised until then just how vital it was. Nothing can survive without it. Nothing except...

I was walking over to the 'kitchen' when I spotted it. A small straggle of green. It had sprouted by the side of my tent.

My forehead tightened into what I suppose was a frown, and I squinted. Because nothing could grow independently on this torrid hill of dust. It was impossible. Stepping toward the mysterious green entity, I expected it to transform into a piece of cable, or hose. But no. Contrary to all reason, something appeared to be thriving. Alone. In a desert.

Scratching my head, I pondered on this little plant. It wasn't pretty, with straggly, dirty green leaves. So I walked away, back to the kitchen. Yet, en route I was astounded to see a few more of them. And the more I looked, the more I saw. Green shrivels were burgeoning all over the place. But how?

While the kettle boiled, I climbed in the hammock under Grandmother Olive, and began to rock. The other, more scraggy olive tree the hammock was tethered to twisted gently as I swung. A cascade of twittering dropped from the trees. Oh, how I loved that spot!

"How is that plant surviving? There's not a drop of water anywhere!" I whispered to Grandmother Olive.

I could smell the warm wood, and the aroma of the pines further up on the ridge. There was a rustle above my head, and the agama's tail flashed above me. Air moved over my arms in soft waves. The pulse of the cicadas throbbed. And suddenly we were all one entity again. The land and I were in sync.

"Is that plant something to do with *me*?" I asked quietly, because that's what now occurred to me.

But then I heard the kettle scream. I saw steam belching out of its spout. Groaning, I yanked myself out of the hammock, and back into my routine.

***

It was in the afternoon, I noticed another sprig of the weed cluttering about the tiny grape-vine remnant I was trying to salvage. The one Celal and Dudu had called a "trick grape". Now, in midsummer, a few cricket-harried leaves clung desperately onto existence.

When I spied the new weed hustling my grape vine and stealing its water, I was suddenly very annoyed.

"Take it!"

I looked up to see Dirt Woman, arms crossed, lips set in a matter-of-fact line. She seemed taller than usual today, and had adopted the dignified stance of a tribal chief.

"Take it!" she repeated.

I looked back at the weed, and my first grape-baby. BAM! In one quick snatch I'd uprooted the plant. I threw it to one side. Or rather I tried to throw it, because it was sticky, secreting something.

"What? What in hell *is* it?"

Dirt Woman moved closer, so close I could smell her sweat. But that wasn't all I was smelling. The plant, which was still stuck to my palm, was emitting a powerful fragrance. I sniffed at the leaves and the stem. It was a cross between lavender and eucalyptus. Taking a deep breath, I sensed something physiological happen when I inhaled.

"This one have good smell. Good for *you*."

"What do I do with it?"

"Put in cold water. You see."

"Water?"

"Yeah. Water."

And then an idea floated into my head. "Is it some sort of aromatherapy?" I asked my earthy friend.

Dirt Woman raised the hedge of one eyebrow and tilted her head questioningly.

"Aromatherapy is when you use plant oils to make you feel better."

My mud accomplice let out a loud sigh, her thick brown lips settling into a pout. "Why you need all this long word? I don't know arom-thruppy. I know living!" She then spat on the floor in exasperation, before turning back to face me. "Your way no good! You know many word but you don't know any *real* thing! You know arom-thruppy, but you don't know you hold medicine in your hand!"

It was of course a completely valid point. Oh, the intellectual babble of the modern human! And with the onslaught of the internet, our knowledge only increases, while our actual experience and wisdom shrivels.

As I stared out across my land, I saw the forest swaying. It was an emerald kingdom of life and initiations, a cauldron of textures, smells, colours and tastes, a home, a community, an apothecary, a playground, a school, and a temple. Laid over this mysterious wonderland, I saw the cage of my language and education: stems, stalks, petals, bifurcation, folioles, stipules, petioles, blades, flowers, stamen, stigma, nodes, internodes, tap roots, lateral roots. Because I could point at something and call it a pine cone, did it mean I understood it?

The answer, of course, was no.

Twisting the strange new plant between my thumb and forefinger, I mused on how to use it. The sun was high in the sky now, an implacable blazing monster. Feeling the sweat running down my back, I found a five-kilogram yoghurt pot I'd collected from a friend, and filled it with water. I placed the plant in the shade of my bathroom and let it soak.

Ten minutes later, I washed my face, neck and arms in the weed water. Oh, the coolness! The soothing freshness of it! Immediately, I was swept up by well-being. It was refreshing. Cleansing. And most extraordinary of all, it dissipated all glumness. Pulling the weed out of the bottom of the pail, I stared at it wide-eyed, because it really did look as though my land had bestowed me with some sort of psychic balm.

I sat for a moment, allowing this breath of herbal magic to waft through me. Then I quickly scoured the land for more of the plant. Once my eyes had grown accustomed to it, I saw it was everywhere.

After that, each evening and morning I washed in my magical plant, feeling yet more new life enter me as I did so. The motorways of my mind turned into country lanes winding gracefully through meadows of flowers. Peace filled me. I found balance.

***

"What is it?" I asked.

Dudu turned my sticky plant round and round in her henna-stained hand. She brought it up to her nose and sniffed, then scrunched her forehead down, clearly unimpressed.

"I don't know what it is, but I don't like it," she said, and threw it over her shoulder. Celal was still sniffing his sprig, his face noncommittal.

"Smelly weed. Aye, thass what it is, slike dopey weed, and that radish weed and this is smelly weed."

"You're making it all up! Smelly weed! Who's ever heard of that?" Dudu scowled at Celal. He tucked the sprig behind his ear and chuckled.

"It cleared up my heat rash and makes me feel so happy. I think it's medicinal." I sniffed my sprig lovingly. Celal and Dudu both studied me in quiet bemusement. Dudu shifted from one foot to the other, Celal picked up his spade.

"And there must be other special plants, right?"

Dudu's face scrunched up, her eyes burrowing into her eyebrows. After a moment's thought, she straightened her headscarf and puffed out her chest. "Well, we do use this one, don't we, Celal?" She pointed at another bush which seemed to thrive in the heat. The one Celal had spared all those months ago. It was an island of green in my yellow desert.

"Aye. Some folks do." Celal lowered his brows a little sceptically.

"*I* use it." My neighbour haughtily squared her shoulders. "You can wrap it found your finger when you cut it and it makes it better. Look." Without further ado, she tore off a leaf of the plant and thrust it in my face. It possessed an acrid smell, not in any way pleasant like my smelly weed. Pulling the leaf back, she wrapped it around her index finger and held it in place.

"If I cut my finger, I Sellotape it on like that and leave it all night, I do. And when I wake up, it's all better," Dudu said.

I raised my eyebrows and blinked. "*Sellotape?*" I studied the digit with the leaf wrapped around it, its fleshy creases daubed in red. It's a custom in Turkey to dye the palms and inner fingers with henna at weddings, so I assumed someone in the village must have got married recently.

"Whose wedding did you go to?" I asked.

"No one's," Dudu said. "I like putting henna on, softens my hands and heals all the scratches, it does." She opened her russet palm a little shyly and peered at it briefly before snapping it shut again. Then she remembered something. The whites around her irises expanded.

"Oh, think about winter!"

"Winter?"

174

"In winter, there's stuff all over you can eat. I'll show you," Dudu slapped me on the arm excitedly. Her eyes turned decidedly occult.

"But are there any more medicines?"

My little neighbour screwed her eyes up and began scanning left and right along my land. Soon she bounced over to a space just behind my tent and snapped a thin twig off. "This one is sage. You can boil it all up in a pot, and make tea out of it. It's good for women's problems."

"Oh yes, I know sage."

"Aye, and there's one for a bad heart. Juss a minute. I seen that one over 'ere somewhere." Celal, not one to be left out, scrambled up to Dudu's fence and began searching in the undergrowth. He was a small, cap-wearing ferret.

"Here it is!"

I clambered up the mound after him and gaped down at his feet. There was a very pale green plant, a little like oregano but whiter and with smaller, thicker leaves.

"Don't eat it though cos it can give you a bad stomach if you eat too much of it."

"So how does it help your heart?"

"Dunno," Celal shrugged unhelpfully.

"You boil it up and drink it!" Dudu shouted up at us. "You have to know how to do it though, or it can kill you." She looked even smaller from our elevated position up on the ridge, a crone hobbit huddled in striped orange şalwars and a grass-stained blouse. Out of the corner of my eye, I spotted the witch in Dudu. She made potions, owned a cauldron, and looked alarmingly like the hag from Hansel and Gretel at times. And there was no denying when it came to all things green, Dudu was wise.

"'S not the only plant that'll kill yer. This bugger 'ere with the black berries..."

"Deadly nightshade," I said.

"Dunno, we call 'em fox grapes."

"No we don't, they're called dog grapes," Dudu called from below.

175

This was typical. One plant seemed to parade under at least six names which changed depending on where the person came from. Later on I looked in the dictionary. Deadly nightshade could be called *wolf grape, fox grape* and *dog grape*. It was also known as *wild jasmine,* and finally there was the inevitable reference to the dangerous female archetype: *beautiful wife weed* and *pretty lady flower.*

I eyed the cluster of black berries Celal was pointing at and gulped. The fate of Ian McCandless drifted out from my memory banks and into the light of day. Yes, the plant kingdom was a gauntlet for the uninitiated and unwitting. Excited as I might be to experiment in the apothecary of my land, I needed a guide.

A beeping sound broke up Yapraklı village's first botany club meeting.

"Oh, that'll be Mehmet, hang on a minute." To my surprise, Dudu hitched up her blouse a little and began unrolling something from the elastic of her şalwars. Her mobile phone. She noticed my astonishment. "Ah, best place to keep it, better than a pocket, never falls out." Then she pressed the green answer key.

Not So Sacred Geometry

"Okay, Celal, we're going to make a shed."

"A shed?" Celal sat on a rock opposite me on our new breakfast balcony, while I glugged down my last swig of coffee. The edges of the air were already sun-baked, and I felt the first beads of sweat collecting around my hairline.

"Yup. For my tools. I'm copying the tent-shade methodology I learned from Evren." I tapped my nose with my index finger and nodded at him. "We'll do exactly the same but make it smaller."

"Alright. Aye, will be good to lock yer stuff up before some bugger comes and nicks it." Celal grabbed the rim of the stool and stood up. He was wearing a pair of grey beach shorts. They were huge on him, and his calves jutted out from the bottoms like two brown twigs. "Where you gonna put it?"

"Over there." I pointed to the very back of the land, just below the ridge. "We'll bring the wood from the roof of the car first, and then we'll get started. Can you help me carry my water tanks too? I'm dead-tired."

Celal smiled. He was standing by one of the other olive trees, the loopy, swirly, messy one. Pulling one of the branches toward his face, he studied the baby olives blooming on it. "This trees bin grafted. These olives are gooduns."

"Really? Not trick ones?" I stepped over to have a look. The small green fruit bobbed as I grabbed the branch.

"Whatcha gonna do about water?" Celal said suddenly. "I say you should pump it up from the canal. Thass what the English did. Made a pool with reeds, they did. The reeds clean the water."

I focused my gaze on Celal in interest. It was a good idea. A brilliant idea in fact. The only trouble was that the canal was a good hundred metres below me. "You'll need to speak to the canal supervisor though, cos you have to pay to use it. They don't give that water to any bugger. And you need electricity. Not sure a petrol pump'll have the guts to get the water up 'ere."

I felt myself literally deflate. Expense. Electricity. And worst of all, some irritating fellow with a title I'd have to bribe, or sweet-talk. I pushed the water issue from my mind. It was just too great a mountain to climb at the present moment. Mind you, when the month of August is on your Mediterranean doorstep, even standing up is a mountain to climb. I decided to wait for September. Everything good happened in September. The children went back to school, the beach emptied, the air cooled, and the world was a happier place.

Without more ado, Celal and I both made our way up from the breakfast terrace, past my tent, up the rocky path and out onto the track. My Fiat stood there coated in a layer of dust, wood protruding from every window. There were boards tied to the roof rack and piled up on the back seat too. I'd had to drive one-handed down the road, because the other arm was holding back the 5-by-10s which ran from the passenger seat and jutted out of the rear window.

Westerners will of course be horrified by this hazardous flouting of health and safety regulations. I will no doubt receive comments from countless well-meaning folk, telling me I really didn't ought to do that, and I need safety gear and gloves and a mask. The thing is, this is Turkey. Such antics are just another day at the mall. And I like living in a country where people don't blindly follow the rules, but bend them, warp them, and step round them. I also like living a little dangerously. It keeps me awake.

Celal and I untied the wood from the roof rack. Then we slid the boards onto the ground. One by one, we pulled the 5-by-10s out of the rear window. Celal threw two of them over his shoulder and started walking down the path. Bending down, I eased a post on to my shoulder, discerned the weight, and then added a second. Feeling the wood digging into my neck, I slowly descended the path.

As I walked, I sensed how much energy I had. I was six months away from forty. Mid-life. Everything was supposed to decelerate from now on, wasn't it? According to common belief, the body had now reached the apex of its mortal journey and was now beginning the downward shuffle into decline. Only something strange had happened. I wasn't losing power, I was gaining it, and my strength and stamina were rising. Fast. It was as if the hands on my biological clock had started moving in reverse, as if someone somewhere had tuned my engine up, upgraded my electrical circuits, and was running me on rocket fuel. This was just as well. I had plenty to do.

"Celal, can you bring the rest of the smaller planks? I'll get some string and a tape measure. We'll peg the string into a square and then we'll see clearly where the posts are going."

Celal squinted at me. I could almost see the question mark sprouting out of his rucked forehead. String? Tape measure? What's that got to do with a shed? He said nothing though and dutifully strode out of the land to complete the ferrying of materials. It was just gone nine by the time we tackled the posts.

Ah...Celal and me and woodwork. When thrown together, those three points formed a triangle of continual frustration – a marginally lopsided triangle which wasn't in any way equilateral, and wobbled when you pushed it. Yes, it was to be a long and difficult relationship we'd share with wood. Over the course of the next two years, we'd utter enough swearwords to graffiti the entire wall of China. And you could have built a Boeing 747 by melting down the nails we bent.

As the sun hammered down on us, Celal dug four holes at the back of the land. I measured the string and set up the square. We both found some flat rocks to support the posts. Celal held the wood and I held the spirit level. The sun drove higher, transmogrifying the land into a slope of white fire. The lizards basked. The pines cracked. The forests became deafening cricket concerts. By lunchtime, tempers were coming loose at the seams.

"Iss straight."

"No it's *not!*"

"'S alright. Didn't do this on my hut and thass still standin' innit?"

I stood up, pushed my sunglasses back, and yanked my baseball cap down. It took the full width and breadth of my restraint not to comment on that hut. Celal's house defied every mathematical principle in the world of geometry. It was a shack from a Brothers Grimm tale, and I had a sneaking suspicion a good fifty per cent of it had been completed with the help of a bottle of raki. Still, I had to admit, despite its unconventional angles, it had survived earthquakes, and hurricanes. So perhaps he was right, and I was being too Western and picky.

"I just want it straight, Celal. Look, hold this right here. Don't move, okay?"

"Okay."

"You *moved*!"

"No I didn't."

"You did! Agh!" I slapped my forehead. "It's wonky now!" And I held up the spirit level to prove the point. Celal's face turned from leather to stone as he pushed the beam forward again.

"Are the nails behind you?"

"Dunno, I ain't got eyes up me arse, have I? If I look round the post'll move."

Then, as was always the case when we were up to our necks in potential failure, Dudu showed up.

"So what are you two up to today then?" She was squatting on a large, lichen-speckled rock overlooking my land. Her observation tower. There was a taciturn silence from the construction team. I gritted my teeth. Celal looked briefly at the floor, then acquiesced.

"'S gonna be a shed." He looked up and the post moved for the umpteenth time. I closed my eyes and let my arm drop.

"Ooh *lovely*, you could do with a shed, Kerry, couldn't you?"

I managed to squeeze a smile out from somewhere. It spurted parsimoniously from the corners my mouth like the very last smidgeon of toothpaste from the tube. I couldn't decide if Dudu was oblivious, or fully aware and fancied stirring a little.

"Why did you make it so small though? You need it double the size, I'm telling you. And that post isn't straight, Celal, I can see it from here." I turned round to see her, a cheeky headscarf-wearing gnome, knees raised, bottom resting on her rock, grinning from ear to ear. I turned back and met Celal's eye. We both crumbled in laughter. Well, what else could we do?

It was at that very moment that the muezzin began the call to prayer. His voice drifted over the hills from Yapraklı mosque, rising and falling with the wind. It was lunchtime. And it hadn't come a moment too soon.

"Oof! Saved by the muezzin. Glad he's doing *something* useful for his two thousand lira a month," said Celal. He let go of the post. It leaned haphazardly over in the hole like a drunken cadet.

***

It took us three days to complete the shed. I had to hire Celal twice in one week, and his wage was paid by my painted stones. We huffed and grumbled at each other. I couldn't count the times we hammered a plank in place only to prise it off a minute later because it was wonky or the wrong way round. It was three solid days of torture by carpentry, and I began to fear that by the end of it that Celal might not come back.

"Don't like this wood lark. Iss too fiddly. And you get right cranky with me." Celal scowled as he pulled out yet another nail.

Fortunately, things improved once the posts were fixed straight. We angled the 10-by-1 boards and banged them horizontally to create a surprisingly sturdy box. At the time, I thought I'd overshot the wood, and spent a couple of years regretting it, because I could have made do with cheaper wood cut-offs from the yard (it was only a shed after all). But five years later I was looking at that shed and feeling nothing but pride. It was our first structure, and probably one of our better woodwork creations. It's certainly the sturdiest and longest-lasting. It'll survive another ten years at least if it's protected regularly. And even Dudu had to admit, we made a pretty job of it.

Soon after, I painted the wood so that the shed was weatherproof, before adding something I'd been longing for ever since I was a kid. By now I was hammering like a professional. So I bought a piece of strand board cut to size, and nailed it into the back wall of the shed. Then I hammered more nails into the surface, leaving them half-banged in to act as hooks. Finally, I hung all my tools up: spirit level, hammer, paint brushes, screwdrivers. It wasn't quite as impressive as some sheds I'd seen. It was small, and I possessed but a limited amount of hand tools. But I loved it nonetheless.

"All you need to do now is make a bigger one. And that can be your house!" Dudu was sitting under Grandmother Olive, fanning herself one day. Despite the late hour the sky was still nuclear, a white bombardment of heat and nothing else. We huddled beneath the shelter of leaves like an unlikely pair of air-raid escapees.

"I don't want a house, Dudu! I love my tent." I gazed lovingly over at all fifty bucks' worth of my canvas blue dome. The tent might have been lurking in the bargain bins at Carrefour, but it was holding up just fine despite the battery of ultraviolet it was subjected to.

"But you can't live in a tent forever!"

"I can! And I will. Walls and roofs are for losers." I folded my arms over my chest, and felt my eyeballs fixing themselves in my eye sockets, obstinacy drawing a line in the dirt.

Dudu's features crumpled a little at the edges. "What about winter?" she said, pushing her lips out.

"What about it?" I answered in gruff conclusion. It was an unfortunate gauntlet to throw myself. Because I had completely forgotten what winter was like.

Mud Magic

I wandered to the opening of my tent, unzipped it, and threw my rucksack inside. Then I turned around to take in the view. The rim of the sun had just disappeared below the mountain ridge on the right, and once again the colours transmuted. An enormous August bug landed on one of the terrace rocks. It was larger than my fist, with a thick woody torso, metallic wings, and eyes the size of small peas. This Turkish cicada was something from Lewis Carroll's imagination. Two months ago, I'd have probably shrunk back at the sight of it. But now? It looked magical. A fantasy creature.

I stared at the insect. Turning toward me, he slowly flapped his wiry wings and I smiled because he looked like he was waving at me. Dropping onto my stomach, I studied him closer. Cicadas are ancient with a lineage stretching back a good 250 million years. They are also widely recognised as the most efficient sound producers in nature (in terms of volume compared to size). Unlike crickets and grasshoppers, they don't rub body parts together to make a noise. Instead, they possess tymbals in their abdomens which vibrate like a rapidly-beaten drum, their exoskeleton acting as an echo chamber and enhancing the sound.

What was it like to be a cicada? Their racket was intense enough to listen to, even for a relatively sound-challenged human. This creature was a living drum with half its life spent vibrating. As I lay there gawping, the cicada's eyes wheeled backwards in my direction. He didn't move. And I couldn't escape the feeling that just as I was studying him, he was studying me.

Slowly, I pulled back and stood up. The cicada's wings buzzed. He flew over my tent toward the forest, a whirring miniature UH-1 helicopter.

Eyes peeled for wonder, I walked over to my hammock. Grandmother Olive was magnetic. She drew me closer and closer. Pulling the rope mesh toward me, I sat on the edge and swung. Such a happiness clutched my heart, I bordered on ecstatic. As I lay back and let the hammock rock, every sorrow evaporated. Tears of gratitude filled my eyes. The branches curled toward me. The rocks tilted in. And I realised I was in love. Really. This was it.

"This tree so good."

I looked up to see my dirt woman curled into the boughs in simian snugness. Her knees were by her chin, while her arms dangled. The matted whorls of her hair draped over her like woolly tentacles. I jerked up in my hammock.

"What are you doing over this side? This tree freaks you out. Last time you touched her you nearly had a heart attack."

"That different. You can hear special word now, because I no scared you run away."

"What special words?" I asked.

She moved away from the trunk and scuttled further along the thick olive branch. Then, wrapping her legs around the gnarly beam, she hung down much like a kid in a playground. Her face was now next to mine, though it was upside down, her hair dropping into my belly. "You want to hear about tree?"

"Of course I do!" I rested my head back on the hammock in anticipation, stretching my hands behind my head and linking the fingers. Grandmother Olive's thick foliage looked unusually lustrous, the tight, thin leaves turning under the sun.

"All tree on this land have a special work, like all plant and animal. But all tree take message from Sky to Earth. They get much idea about coming time and before time in their root and they message all land. They talk much. Tree very special.

"What do you mean they all have a special job?" I said. "Are you telling me there's a career's office in the forest?"

"All thing in nature have special job. 'S natural. All thing fit and work with all other thing in nature. I say before we are family. This true. This land is small family. And the many small family make big family."

"I see."

"All tree have different job. Different power. Different...voice. Some help when you ill. Some tell you very good idea. Some hold spirit from Sky, some give energy, and some giving only love. Some make you feel peace. Some protect you or protect land. Some even know future. You must go and sit with all tree. Talk with them. Hear them." From her upside-down position she swept her arm about the land, pointing out the trees.

"I think I knew that somewhere already. I don't know why, but it feels very instinctive."

"Yes! You must know this." Dirt Woman's upside-down features stretched outwards. "You part of forest and earth. You made from same thing!" Her abdominal muscles flexed, and she retracted up to the branch as nimbly as a lemur. Pulling herself up, she scampered back to the trunk.

Unwrapping my hands, I peered up and saw her, back resting against Grandmother Olive's thick stem. Her eyes were closed. Her features were soft. A faint smile graced her lips. She simply sat there, communing with the tree, looking as peaceful and content as a house-cat by an open fire.

I followed her lead. Well, why not? What did I have to do that was so important anyway? Relaxing in the hammock, I let Grandmother Olive wash over me. The cicadas hummed. The sunlight danced through the olive leaves. And I surrendered to it. Briefly, I wondered what would happen if I did absolutely nothing all day.

Time passed. More time followed. Every muscle in my body was soft, every cell humming happily. A quiet type of bliss suffused through me and beyond me, until I couldn't really tell where I ended and the land began. It was perfect.

As day crossed the sacred boundary into night, I gazed toward the forest. The pines thrust their limbs upwards, twigged fingers reaching for the sky. And I knew they were organic antennae picking up signals from The Beyond. The forest absorbed those messages. It held them. And now that I was initiated, I decided I was going to listen to them.

***

Trees have been around eons. The now extinct Gilboa trees found in upstate New York are the first we know of, and they appeared about 380 million years ago. They were peculiar trees, neither woody nor leafy and grew vaguely like a long, bendy palm. Since then trees have been evolving, growing, facing extinction, and adapting.

Is anything on the planet quite as beneficent as the tree? We live on their oxygenated air, we are nourished by their fruits, nuts, leaves and oils, we construct our dwellings from their wood, utilize their bark, cork, resins, and latex. They provide us with wood to burn, shade to hide under, and their sturdy root systems prevent erosion. Trees attract clouds and precipitation, create wind breaks, generate mulch, and create homes for all kinds of other life; spiders, ants, birds, gekkos, snakes, squirrels, to name but a few. And in terms of aesthetic, their architecture is unsurpassed.

But this is only the tangible side of the tree. Because our arboreal cohabitants on this planet are not simply a resource or a product. They are a living, respiring miracle.

"Come. Come with me." Dirt Woman was standing at the edge of the forest one morning, finger crooked. It was still early. The copper lid of the sun had only just been lifted, and the bisque of the sky was laced with lilac.

I threw my comb into my tent and trotted toward her. As I left the sun-chafed slope and moved into the trees, I shivered, because there's nowhere quite like a forest.

A network of skinny paths snuck through the thicket, and the bosky alleyways of dry needles and broken twigs cackled as we trod through them. Pines towered above us, their crusty great trunks jacking up the sky, while smaller trees and shrubs crowded underneath this living marquee.

The further into the forest we walked, the deeper the mulch became, until I was sinking up to my calves in cones and needles.

"This one. Here." Dirt Woman grabbed my hand and pulled me forward. I squeezed past a rock, and carefully unpicked a thread of briars that had wound itself around my knee. Finally, I was free. I looked up and gasped. Here, hidden from everyone, submerged in the very heart of the forest, was a carob tree. The branches curled in capacious arcs forming a cupola of glossy leaves. Bundles of carobs dangled like dark, shrivelled hands.

Like the olive, the carob is far more magnanimous than she appears. Despite her withered wood and weak limbs, she's a generous tree that thrives in tough conditions. The copious carob pods can be eaten, or ground down into powder and used as a healthy sugar substitute. Donkeys and goats love them too. But the ultimate delicacy is the molasses created by boiling the pods for days in water. A thick black treacle is produced which is rich in iron, and deliciously sweet.

Stepping beneath the tree, I stretched my hand out and stroked her trunk.

"Many tree like this around our land. They make a…" Dirt Woman paused, splayed the fingers on both her hands, and placed one over the other to form a lattice.

"A web? There's a web of carobs? Ah…I see, you mean a network of them in this area."

"Yes. All are family. And all talk to each other. They watch all time."

"Like guardians? Or watchkeepers?"

"Yes. They look after here, and watch people who come here. I show you one more. Very special one. Grandfather tree."

Dirt Woman leaned forward and kissed the carob's trunk, then stealthily crept back up through woodland, while I clambered ungainly in pursuit. When we reached the upper tracts near my land, I stopped for a minute. It was beautiful in there, a quiet dappled enclave. And unlike my land, which perched like a castle on a hilltop, the forest was hidden from everyone. Finches twittered, jays squawked, and any number of bugs buzzed. It was a world within a world, and I wondered if I could create a space here, a space to read and be inspired.

We threaded up the dusty path to the track by the fearsome forest. I followed my dirt-dwelling accomplice along the forest edge. The track ended abruptly in a glade. I knew this place well. The land looked straight onto the crown of Mount Olympos, the highest peak in the region, and I had walked here frequently, because it was such a beautiful spot. But its most impressive feature was slap-bang in its centre. It held the most incredible carob tree I've ever seen.

The tree was huge, so large you could have easily fit twenty people under it. The branches arced over the ground in an enormous umbrella, and the gnarled arms formed a spacious shelter. It was a living, leafy version of my dome tent, only much, much bigger.

Dirt Woman disappeared under the boughs, and I followed suit, spotting the red brush of a squirrel darting up into the highest branches.

"This the grandfather. He very...he know many thing about old time and new."

"He's wise," I said. "I can feel it too. I shall call him the Wisdom Carob."

"You come here and ask question. If you open your ear and eye and heart, you hear answer." Dirt Woman stroked the enormous double trunk of the tree. It was full of holes and niches, and I could feel it drawing me in. Walking up to the trunk, I laid my hand on the bark. The carob was smoother than a pine or an olive, and felt more like dry leather.

It was then I did something I hadn't done in thirty years. Sticking one hand in one of the niches, and grabbing a branch with the other, I climbed the tree. Soon I was sitting within the ample boughs. It was so quiet up there. And so warm. I'd forgotten how wonderful it felt to huddle within the arms of a tree.

As I sat there, I suddenly became aware that this was a power point. A centre. The area felt like a natural ward which included my land and Dudu's, the three forests, and stretched about two kilometres from Adnan's house to the canal. It was a terrain for which this tree was some sort of custodian.

"This tree talk with all other brown pod tree. They guard here. If the tree no like you, you no stay." Dirt Woman dropped to the ground at this point and laid in the mulch like a starfish. "When you rest here, you learn many thing," she added before closing her eyes.

And as I reclined in the massive arms of this incredible tree, I closed my eyes too. The life inside the wood was palpable. A subtle breeze threaded through the upper branches, and thousands of thick ripe carobs clattered together. The tree was a giant rattle, and I could sense there was indeed some secret here, some arcane knowledge encrypted in its fibres. But I couldn't yet tell what it was.

***

If the tree no like you, you no stay.

Overactive imagination. New-age fluff. Hogwash, right?

Over the next few years, I would witness many strange things occurring within the Wisdom Carob's province. One of them was related to who could and who couldn't manage to build a property in our neighbourhood. As I wandered all over the area, I began to stumble upon ruins. Eerie ruins. These were not the remnants of ancient cities, but rather the vestiges of modern foundations or even sometimes entire houses. They were structures people had tried to build here and failed. The odd thing was there were so many of them! In fact, there were more abandoned constructions lurking in the undergrowth than there were completed houses.

Interestingly, most of these neglected structures had been commissioned by the wealthy. They had been abandoned because the owners were stopped in their tracks somehow. Perhaps they failed to obtain permission for water, quite a few times some odd calamity had befallen them (the number of untimely deaths in the area was more than a little spooky). All in all it made you wonder. Why did some people manage to make a home here, and others didn't?

Years later, after much investigation and thought, one commonality emerged. All those who succeeded in creating a home in the Wisdom Carob's ward had camped on their property first: Dudu, Zeynep, the other English.

What difference should that make? Living in a tent for months on your land changes your entire relationship with it. The land knows. The trees know. The animals know. The Wisdom Carob knows.

And now in the future, I observe the fear and greed-based madness of big business, the utter disregard for the soul of the planet and the non-human life forms upon her, the incredible way many humans are willingly sacrificing their freedom and power for technological conveniences, the bombing of children in the Middle East, the mass extinctions, and the decimation of our forests. It looks fairly hopeless.

But it's not. Not quite. Because there is one thing most humans seem to have forgotten. The planet is not a passive observer. She is alive. She is responsive. And no one, not even the cartel of the world's richest, understand what life really is, or how it works.

The rationalists snort at talk of the soul of the planet. And the pessimists and whiners in the environmental community do too. Multinational business owners don't care. But as I consider that some of Turkey's richest and most well-connected had failed to construct houses on that beautiful stretch of Lycia, while I with my paltry $6000 managed to manifest a mud paradise, I begin to understand. Power isn't money. It's something else.

The Rationalist

"Whoa! Nice pad." Adnan patted my tent, while I pushed a wheelbarrow with a tank of water in. It slopped and slurped as the barrow struck rocks and roots and holes. I must have looked a little incongruous. I was wearing a red summer dress, jewellery, and wellington boots. The wellies were because I was down to my last pair of sandals and didn't want to wreck them.

"Is the live band any good?"

"Yup. If they were playing in Europe they'd be charging 30-euro-a-head entrance fee." This was true. Café Cactus had a knack for drawing highly-talented musicians from Istanbul to play in the bar during the summer. Adnan and I were heading for a night out in the valley, which was why I was dressed up. Adnan's jet black hair was slicked back. He was wearing jeans and pumps, and had a black daypack slung over his shoulder. He looked about twenty-five.

"Jeez! Aren't you like shit-scared of the insects?" Adnan's eyes scanned the terrain, and grew wide. "I saw the scorpion from hell in my toilet yesterday. I flushed and flushed but it just kept coming at me, like the goddamn terminator. Oh *man*, they are so creepy!"

Bringing my barrow to a standstill by the kitchen, I looked up at Adnan and chuckled. He'd negotiated Iraq, Afghanistan, and Pakistan multiple times, spent intense minutes staring into the barrels of AK47s, and was bombed in Baghdad. But show him a scorpion, and the man started running. Still, everyone's scared of something. Later I'd be very glad of Adnan's immunity to gun fear. The day a trigger-happy nutcase began prowling the perimeter of my land, I'd be in awe of his unfazed nonchalance in the face of a firearm or two.

Adnan walked over to my kitchen and began tapping the pans and wooden spoons hanging from the gnarled branches of the wild oak. They swung on their twiggy hooks, creaking gently.

"So are you going to get water and power, or stay like this forever?"

"I'm not connecting to the grid. Screw the lot of them!" I said, quickly recalling my chat with the headman. "You know the beauty of this? I've realised I don't need the government. It's crazy when you think about it, charging us for water. No other being on the planet has to *pay* to drink and wash."

Heaving the water canister from the wheelbarrow, I groaned and dumped it on the earth next to my makeshift worktop. It had been fashioned out of an old television console, and I stored my crockery in a fruit crate beneath it. Adnan peered down at that crate. Then he stood back up and studied the rest of the kitchen: the dusty gas cylinder on the chest of drawers, the stick and twine washing-up rack, the earth floor.

Standing upright, I pushed the barrow out of the kitchen. It was then I spied something dangling from Grandmother Olive's branches. Something brown and grubby. It swung to and fro in time with the buzz of the evening crickets like a metronome. Peering a little closer, my vision closed in on a brown toenail, a cracked heel. And I realised. Someone was eavesdropping on our conversation.

"What are you gonna do when it rains?" Adnan said, tapping at the dirt floor with the toe of his running shoe.

I tilted my head back so that my cranium touched the top of my spine. Then I gazed up at the sky. It was an open arc of munificence. Pale blue. Dimming to violet. Rain seemed so impossibly far away, I had never bothered to consider it. The days were furnaces. The nights were starry baths. "I don't know to be honest," I admitted, and walked over to Grandmother Olive.

The foot in the branches stopped swinging. It hung there, purposefully still. Poised.

"I think the land is protecting me though," I added, stroking the thick, scratchy bark of the trunk.

Adnan's head jerked up. He elevated one black eyebrow. Then the other. Then lowered them both again.

"I mean, I haven't seen a snake, or a pig, or a scorpion all summer. Isn't it strange?" As I stood with my back to Grandmother Olive's trunk watching Adnan in my kitchen, I sensed movement behind me. The slight hiss of dead olive leaves. A coolness. Out of the corner of my eye I spied Dirt Woman, dreadlocks hanging down, neck craned, onyx eyes nailed on Adnan.

Adnan was oblivious because he was hunched over inspecting my wash rack. "There could be any number of logical reasons for the lack of animals, Kerry," he said, running his index finger over the twigs. "The land isn't a person. It's a thing. I really think we need to stay away from all this new-age crap about Gaia being some sort of conscious being."

I could hear the gnashing of teeth behind me. The low-pitched growl. Not daring to look back, I focused my gaze on the kitchen wondering if I should bother to discuss this. A primitive finger jabbed me directly between the shoulder blades. I sighed and readied myself for battle.

"You don't *know* that the Earth isn't sentient," I blurted. "I mean, how would you prove it?"

"Well, the Earth doesn't have a cerebral cortex or a nervous system for a start. And you need that for consciousness." Adnan had now turned to face me, and I could just tell he was chomping at the bit for a debate. I swung round briefly to face my ancient dirt sister. She linked her hands together to form a bridge from the fingers, and then flexed the palms outward and inhaled competitively. *Oh Lord!* I was a glutton for argument at the best of times. But with Dirt Woman on my back? I dreaded to think.

"Consciousness and thoughts don't occupy physical space, Adnan. You can't apply the laws of physics to something non-physical. That's the trouble with 20th-century thought. It's outdated. Still stuck in three dimensions. Move on from Newton!"

"Thought *is* physical!" Adnan rose to the challenge, eyes gleaming white in the dimming light. "It's happening in your brain. Synapses fire."

"That's not the actual thought though, is it? That's the physical result of the thought."

"No, it's the cause of it."

"You can't prove that. But either way, the chemical reactions, the activity of neurons and synapses; these are *not* the thought. The thought itself occupies no space. It's not a material object."

Adnan's brown irises rose upwards to process this argument. Dirt Woman, sensing a momentary advantage, slapped me on the arm. I turned to see her mouthing "No mercy!" The tips of her incisors were showing, and her thick brows were lowered as she trained her gaze on her prey.

Swinging round to the kitchen again, I decided to defend her. Because, despite her uncouth tactics, I had realised Dirt Woman was onto to something. Something enormous. Something that was changing *my* life. I leaned my right shoulder against Grandmother Olive's trunk and addressed my rational journo-neighbour.

"Okay. Imagine the planet Saturn, right now, swirling in your mind's eye. Where *is* that thought? It's not in your head. It's nowhere. Calculate 4 + 4. Where is that calculation? If I cut your head open, will I find it? Could you ever do any kind of scientific experiment to prove exactly *what* I was seeing in my mind's eye, the actual 'substance' of my imaginings?"

Adnan scratched his chin, and looked over at the land. The light was polished chrome now, and a few sparse blotches of green were glowing. Then he stared back at me. There was a pause. For a moment I could have sworn he caught sight of the dirt woman, or at the very least her shadow, because he shuddered ever so slightly. "Well, even so, none of this means the Earth has a soul," he said.

In my right ear, I heard a chuckle. It was a miniscule victory, perhaps more of a stalemate, but Dirt Woman didn't care.

Adnan and I both walked thoughtfully back to my tent. On reaching the bamboo matting in front of my canvas home, I pulled my feet out of my wellies and slid them into my one surviving pair of sandals. Adnan scanned the rest of the land silently. Kneeling, I pulled my bag from the inside of my tent, and zipped up the door.

"Do you worry about things being stolen?" Adnan said. His rucksack was perched on his back and in the dusk he resembled one of the mutant ninja turtles (more specifically Donatello).

"This is the great thing about being poor. I've nothing to steal," I laughed. And it was true. It was liberating not having a lock, and not possessing anything worth locking. That feeling of freedom was another aspect of my lifestyle that was impacting me. It was a new dimension for me. I don't know if I realised at that juncture quite how significant it was, but over the next few years the quest for utter liberation from the need for money was going to change the direction of my life. It was a holy grail I would search for. A type of promised land.

"Okay, let's hit the road. The valley awaits!" I said finally. We both turned and trotted toward the car. As we walked over the plateau at the top, and up the dusty path, Adnan pulled out a pre-rolled cigarette.

"Why did you ban smoking? Like, what's the deal there? I've seen you sneak the odd roll-up."

Resting my own rucksack – once yellow, now grey-brown and besmirched beyond recognition – on the boot of the car, I paused. It was a question I fielded regularly, and it was a drastic move to take in a country comprising the second-largest number of smokers in the world.

"I made a promise to the land," I answered. "I know you think it's crap, but for me this is a sacred space, a place of protection. My shelter. I just want it to stay pure. Smoking here feels wrong. It's not a moral stance, simply a mark of respect for this space."

"I don't think it's crap. I just like to question things," Adnan said, before turning around from the car to look at the land once more. The pines guarding the east side of the land bristled thickly. Their pointed crowns were living turrets. Over and above them, the sea of the sky glimmered faintly. The slope fell away in a pale yellow rush. It tumbled beyond my boundary, sinking into the cleft of two giant mountains, becoming pomegranate orchards, forests, and hills.

Adnan grinned. "It sure is pretty though. That view is amazing."

The ember at the end of Adnan's roll-up flickered. He puffed one last time before folding the butt in two. I stood up and pulled my bag from the top of the car bonnet. Thrusting the butt of his roll-up in his pocket, Adnan opened the passenger door. Ducking, he slid into the car. I started the engine, nosed her round, and then pressed the gas hard for the familiar high-speed run up the slope.

"Jeez! This road is gonna be interesting in winter," Adnan's right hand pushed against the roof of the car, while his left hand gripped the door handle. The suspension took its regular pounding, as we jolted and banged our way up the dusty incline.

"Yee ha!" I yelped in delight, because for some reason (possibly due to the fact I'm from Essex, a part of the UK famous for its boy racers), as soon as I'm behind the wheel, I turn swiftly and peculiarly into an adolescent male. I fought with the steering wheel as my trusty old Fiat skidded round the potholes, until finally we turned a bend and the track evened out a little.

"Why did you choose this place to live?" I asked as we threaded our way through Yapraklı village. The road was tarmac now, and my car hummed in gratitude.

"I was sick of Istanbul, the city, the pollution, and being in that...you know...'that crowd'. I wanted somewhere peaceful to write."

I nodded. "Yes. It's a good place for a writer. Very...inspiring."

As we began our descent into the valley, the North Star punctured the dimming reality of the sky. She was a shimmering pearl in a fast-dissolving vault. The pines thickened around us as we wound our way round the bends. We crossed the dry river, rock faces leaning over the way like Paleozoic hulks. The road was a black basilisk slipping and sliding from world to world as we rattled over her gravelly scales. Suddenly the mountainsides were above us, not below us. The darkness deepened, and the black holes in the forest dilated. We were back in the Lost City.

Autumn Panic

"I need a platform, Celal!"

"Aye, that yer do. Get that tent off the ground before the rain starts fallin'."

September had arrived. Oh pleasant, affable September. Such a gentleman of a month after the hot, slimy ogre of August. The steam had lifted from the air, and the sky was as crisp and clean as freshly starched cotton. Everything shone in relief – the pines, the rocks, even the finches twittered more easily.

But Celal was right. The change in weather signified the tiptoeing of autumn in our direction. Rain would fall. And if I didn't raise my tent from the ground, I'd soon find myself soggy.

"How we gonna do it?" Celal was still dressed in his baggy grey shorts, his legs jutting from the bottoms like a pair of nobbled twigs. He screwed his eyes up in the early morning sunshine and peered at me inquisitively. We were both standing under Grandmother Olive surveying the area belonging to my tent.

"Well, we'll dismantle the tent shade that Evren made. We'll use four big posts from it and make a rectangle out of them, right there." I pointed from the shade to an empty space near the forest's edge. "Then we'll bang some 10-by-5s around the base.

"You got 10-by-5s?"

"From the tent shade again," I said.

Celal studied the shade and scratched his chin. "There are only six 10-by-5s on that shade," he said.

"Yes, and we only need four for the base." Impatience began bubbling on the stove of my mind. Here we were again. Me, Celal, and wood. It was always a jutting, ill-measured combination.

"And whatcha gonna stick on the platform to walk on and stuff?"

"Planks. And before you ask, they're here. I bought them yesterday," I said, poking a finger indignantly at my wood pile which was sheltered from the sun by two of the kilims I'd bought for the blighted yoga mission at Café Cactus. It was the fate of those kilims never to see a yoga pose, nor even a picnic. They suffered from start to finish in mucky construction work. After two years of covering wood and polypropylene sacks, they finally ended their days on my roof enduring grass roots burying into them.

Celal trotted over to the wood pile, tweaked the rug on the top, and gave the contents a cursory once-over.

"So let's take the shade apart first." I stepped out from Grandmother Olive's cool umbrella, the heat of the morning swiping me hard enough that I lowered my baseball cap. Walking over to one of the tent shade posts, I shook it a little. Then I wandered round to the front of my tent and unzipped the hatch. Crouching in front of the tent flap, I reached inside. In seconds, I was holding my latest and most-coveted possession, a new lithium-charged cordless drill.

"Ah, you gotcha-self a *drill!*" Celal was standing behind me. And I could hear from the syrupy elongation of the vowels, he was drooling. Swivelling round, I clutched the power tool to my chest like a small, blue puppy.

"Yes, it's going to save my life up here. It's great. I can charge it at Dudu's and then use it all day." I stroked it protectively.

Celal moved closer. I took a step backwards.

"Can I look?" he said finally, raising his cap a little. Begrudgingly I released my grip on the drill. Celal cradled it in his hands and turned it over and over, whistling.

"Looks nice. 'S English innit?"

"I don't know. Is it?"

"Yeah, looks English. How much did it cost yer?"

I shuffled and shifted, irritated by these prying money questions always so ubiquitous here in rural Turkey. "It was on sale. Just ninety lira."

Celal pressed the trigger, and the drill bit whirred pleasingly. We both stood for a moment admiring it, before I grabbed it hurriedly back.

"Okay, let's take off the bamboo matting first and then unscrew these posts," I said, pointing the drill at the top of the shade and enjoying its similarity to a revolver. Which is a little paradoxical, because I'm very anti-guns.

***

An hour later, Celal was standing over by the forest, pick in hand, digging a hole. It was the last of four such cavities, each marking a corner of the rectangle that was to become my tent platform. The late morning heat was now sharp and serious, hot yellow shafts driving through the pine trees.

We had dismantled the platform. The bamboo was rolled up and propped against my shed. Six fat posts were scattered on the dust like giant, fallen toothpicks. During their three months of summer service they had of course warped far out of shape, two so bowed at the ends I wondered how we'd use them. One by one, I carried over four of the straightest poles. Then I surveyed our new construction site. The platform was going to be similar to the shed, only this time instead of a roof and walls, I'd be creating a floor.

Staggering with one of the posts, I slotted it in a freshly-dug hole. Celal dropped the pick. "You hold it, an' I'll get some rocks to shove under it," he said and trotted off to scour the back of the land.

Minutes later he was wobbling over to me with a huge flat rock in his arms. He dropped it beside me. It smacked the soil, sending reverberations through me, and countless small, dirt-dwelling creatures.

"Lift the post up."

I raised it a little. Celal dropped to his knees and dragged the rock into the hole. We grunted and sweated and puffed, lifting the post, pushing the rock, until both seemed to be firmly in their place.

"Okay, now let's bang two wooden supports in to hold the post up," I said. "You know, like Evren did with the shade, remember that?"

"Right choo are." Celal galloped to the wood pile amidst the dead grass stubs. From my pole-supporting position, I saw him pull back the green woollen kilim once more. He quickly slid out two reject timber boards left over from the composting toilet project. Standing up, he waved them in the air. It looked a bit like he was directing a plane in to land; a rickety, propeller plane in a country with an economy smaller than Global Motors. Pulling one hand from my post, I raised my thumb at him.

Ten minutes later we'd done it. The support boards were nailed into the post and driven into the ground. The post was now standing all by itself, and was by all spirit-level accounts perfectly vertical. Celal stood up and put one hand on his lower back to stretch. Then he raised the palm of his other hand, ready for a high five. I did my best to strike his hand with my own. It was a little farcical, the Turkish gardener and the English teacher slapping palms like basketball players. Nevertheless, we were ecstatic. We whooped and shouted as though we'd just riveted the crown on to the Eiffel tower.

As we both stood basking in our glory, the mosque struck up the call to prayer. Lunchtime was here. Time for a break. And I wondered. Could it be true? Had Celal and I finally mastered the art of wood?

***

It was afternoon. The sun was fatter and less accommodating now. Food sat in our bellies, draining the blood from our brains. It was always such an effort to recommence after lunch. I found the hours between two and three irritatingly unproductive. The land rolled away from us in flabby, yellow mounds, shored in by the scraggy, wild oaks below.

"Right, hold the string tight. No, *tight*! If it's not tight, it's pointless."

"'S pointless anyway."

Straightening, I funnelled a silent but heated stare at Celal. He was squatting at one of the post bases, with the end of a piece of twine between his brown fingers grinning mischievously.

"If we don't have the twine, it'll be all wonky."

"Dunno about that. You can juss get one of them nice 10-by-1s you bought for the platform deck, and lay it across the back. They're straight."

Celal was in fact right. But I didn't quite see that at this stage in our woodworking relationship. So I raised myself a little higher for added haughtiness.

"We're using the string. And that's that," I said, jerking my head slightly on the second 'that' to indicate the discussion was over.

And this was how the platform-building operation was to progress, both this day, and the next and the next; me as inexperienced as I was perfectionist, Celal countering my every idea. He was a bucking, braying mule that I was trying to push uphill. Except that I wasn't certain which way was up, and the mule knew it.

It was a full week later that we banged the last plank down and my raised wooden deck was complete. The September sun had turned keener, the light so bright I was squinting even with sunglasses on. With the clear-cut peaks of the surrounding mountains as his witness, Celal leapt onto the freshly-nailed floorboards and performed a little jig. But my attention clung to the edges of the platform like a pernickety limpet. The ends of the boards weren't quite lined up in places. And it scratched at my sense of aesthetic.

That evening, once Celal left, I pulled a cushion onto the platform to meditate. The dolphin of the sun dove quickly below the surface of the sea-sky, leaving a trail of pink and gold in its wake. As I sat cross-legged and inhaled, I felt myself submerging too, below the surface of the mind and into the beyond. The smell of pine resin reached my nose. The twitter of the birds was a feathery, living wind-chime. The air cooled. The light changed. And I sensed the life inside my body. Vital. Substantial. Real.

"Why you make wood box? You no like earth now?"

Dirt Woman was back. I grinned because I'd missed her.

"Because I don't want my arse to get wet when it rains," I said. I turned in her direction. Dirt Woman was squatting on the ground in front of my new platform, peering up at me. Her eyebrows were crocheted into a perplexed knot.

"Why you no sleep in the forest? Forest keep me dry."

My ribcage fell as I sighed. I stretched my legs out in front of me, and placed my hands, palms down, behind me as a rest. The sky was dimming now, and the zigzagged line of the mountain ridges was less distinct. Dusk was smudging the boundary between heaven and Earth.

I pondered on Dirt Woman's words. Was my new platform the first act of separating myself from the land? In the quest for comfort and security, we must inevitably sacrifice a part of the connection. And so we forget our footings on our planet. Our trust in the elements. The life force inside us. Drop by convenient drop.

But the truth was, I'd never even considered sleeping in the forest, for another reason.

"I have to stay on my land. It protects me," I said. "The forest isn't mine. It's a wild place."

Dirt Woman stared at me hard. She stood up slowly, arms dangling by her sides like freshly-killed serpents. Her bare skin glimmered slightly in the remnants of daylight, highlighting the sculpting of her muscles. She crooked her finger at me, beckoning me closer. Curious, I slid forward on the platform, until I was sitting on its front edge, legs hanging down.

My friend from the forest leaned forward, bending her head to my left ear. I felt the warmth of her breath as she whispered. Her voice was so quiet, I could hardly pick out the words.

"Scaredy-waredy woman need protecting. Weak woman need protecting. You no weak. This protecting no good for you. It make you like..." she paused, apparently hunting for a word I might understand. "Like something I hunt..."

"You mean victim?" I pulled my head back feeling my face rumple in confusion. And then I blurted, "But I *do* need protecting! There's all kinds of trouble out there!"

The dirt woman shook her head, matted locks shuddering as she did so. "No trouble out there," she said, still hushed. "Trouble in *here*." She jabbed my temple with her index finger. "You make trouble inside, then it comes on outside."

I gawked at her for a moment, and let the idea settle. Scratching my scalp, I considered the trouble in my head. The lists of terrible imaginings. The self-inflicted horror stories. "The thing is, I can't get rid of the trouble in my head. I mean, I'm scared of stuff. That's all there is to it."

"Why no good things in your head? Who put bad things in it? You very strong woman. All man and woman strong. Land and forest know it. You have mind and this has much power. You no need protecting." And with that she poked her index finger into her mouth and began digging around her teeth.

Swinging my legs to and fro, I fell silent. The mountains now formed a dark ring of jagged authority, and for an instant I felt hemmed in. But only for an instant. For night was rising. It flooded the landscape in a wave of pitch, drowning out the peaks in minutes.

Deep down, I knew the Dirt Woman had a point. At any time of day, I could envisage some sort of disaster and sense the fear bloating inside me until I couldn't think straight. It was mysterious that something as ephemeral as a thought could create an emotional energy of that intensity. But was she right? Did the fear actually create *things* to be afraid of? Did it shape reality? Because that's what it seemed she was saying.

But Dirt Woman had already turned from the platform and was padding toward the forest. She swivelled her head round once more before she disappeared. "Remember, you no be afraid!" she hissed, and slid into the arms of the pines.

Reciprocal Roof

There is a wonderful structure in the world of natural building called a reciprocal roof. One of the benefits of the design is that there is no central pole to hold the ceiling up. It's an entirely self-supporting structure. It's also a perfect example of a mutually supportive system, where each beam and rod in the roof upholds the one in front, and is in turn propped up by the one behind. The roof rods then fan out from the centre and are attached to the neck of a circular wall. There's some evidence that the Celts used reciprocal roofs in their roundhouses, which sits nicely with their more cooperative and less hierarchical social structure. Whether or not it was true, I liked the idea.

It was about three o'clock and the pine trees were rocking noisily from an easterly wind. Celal and I were standing behind my tent platform, gawping up at its top. Until now, all construction had been down to the pair of us. But as must be all too clear, our two-pronged A-frame of a team was sorely lacking a truss. So how fortunate that one had just appeared on the ridge of the land to contribute a bit of rigor.

"So what are you gonna do to the roof? I mean, it needs a shade, right?" Adnan bounced down the path and stopped beside us, craning his neck. His jet hair gleamed in the afternoon light, and I could just tell he was itching to get involved. Because natural building is like that. It sucks people in. This doesn't happen on mainstream building sites. Who wants to mess about with steel girders and inhale chemicals and concrete dust? No. The volunteer builder is a mud, wood, and stone phenomenon.

"Hmm, I'm not sure." Then I translated for Celal, "What kind of roof are we going to make?"

"Stick some of 'em straight buggers up there. Run 'em from back to front, juss like the other one." Celal squinted from under his cap. His entire face was screwed up like a crumpled ball of baking paper. Gone were his shorts. He was dressed in over-sized jeans again. September was drawing to a close. It was still a good 30 degrees, but for us, habituated to the 45-degree sauna of summer as we were, it almost felt nippy.

"I saw a reciprocal roof in Fethiye," I said. "It was on a platform just like this. May be we could make one."

"Yeah! Awesome! We should try that." Adnan dropped his rucksack on a rock, and rolled up his sleeves, clearly au fait with the roofing style.

I translated as best I could for Celal. But he was perturbed. Hunching up his shoulders, he peered suspiciously out from under his cap peak. "Never seen one of them. What do we need for it?" he asked, grudgingly.

"Well, the one I saw was made with tree branches. It looked really nice."

This was to be my first encounter with the alarming actuality that Celal hated doing anything new. If he was working within the parameters of his experience, he was happy. If not, he became tense and flustered. And this was unfortunate, because I thrive on the new and untried, and am never happier than when I'm pioneering.

"Alright then. I'll go cut some straight branches. Dunno about the rest though." Celal grabbed the machete, and off he ambled, huffing and grumbling into the woods.

"Man! This is great! So how are we gonna do this thing?"

"Lord knows!" I chortled. "I've never had a clue how I'm going to do anything up here. I think you have to rest the sticks all on top of each other so they form a circle in the middle, and I seem to remember my friend telling me you need to nail the first one to an upright pole, and then when it's all together you take the pole out."

"Okay. I think we should make a prototype first though, hey, Kerry?"

Prototype? My eyes widened and my chin lowered. This was a new concept to me. Scanning my creations – the composting toilet, the shed, and the spanking-new tent platform – I realised I'd never once engaged in anything as sensible as a model. I was always too excited just to get my teeth into the build. But Adnan wasn't a rash rash fly-by-night builder. He was methodical.

"It would be great to make a tiny version here while Celal is finding the larger branches," he said. "You have any smaller sticks?"

"Yup, I've got plenty. Right here." Kneeling, I scooped out a pile of dry canes from under the tent platform, and they clattered into the sunlight. Adnan and I picked out the straightest rods, and swiftly fanned them out on the dirt like sunrays.

"Okay, so what's the next step in the technique?" Adnan scratched his chin.

"Erm, well they have to rest one on top of the other like this." I bent down and placed one stick over the next, and then placed the next in the circle over that. "I suppose the last one tucks under somehow," I said, having but the vaguest of ideas how that might pan out.

"But there must be some kind of measurement, right?" Adnan had screwed his eyes up and was assessing my idea dubiously. I blinked at him, then opened and closed my mouth a few times like a wayward carp. I mean yes, I suppose there *must* have been some rule for measuring, some sort of reciprocal formula that people who like that type of thing spend hours, calculator in hand, geeking over. But all those numbers and equations were just too dull for me to wade through. Where was the challenge? So I shrugged in response. And that shrugging felt good. It was a shrugging off of rules and regulations and systems and the like that continues to upset perfectionists, doctrinaires, and health-and-safety Nazis to this very day.

"Hold this a minute," I said. And Adnan bent down to grasp the first stick that the others were resting on. Then one by one, I placed the rest of the canes, one on top of the other, until the circle was almost complete. Finally I tucked the last stick under the first one. A reciprocal structure appeared.

"Hey, that's good," said Adnan. "Should I let it go?"

"Yes, let's see what happens." I stood back.

Adnan released the supporting rod. Promptly the sticks slid back in the dirt, and the entire structure collapsed with a rattle and a scrape. "Uh oh."

"It's because they're not fixed on the bottom," I said.

"Yeah, I agree. We really need to attach them to something."

But before we could take more action, our experiment was bust apart by another clatter. Celal dropped a heap of large freshly-cut branches onto the ground behind of us.

"Wow!" Adnan stared up at Celal in wonder.

"Yes, brilliant, Celal!" I sprang to my feet and grinned. Where Celal had procured these amazing branches from was anyone's guess, and I suspected it was better not to ask. Nonetheless, we now had some beautifully straight branches for our reciprocal roof project.

***

Two hours later I had my reciprocal roof. It wasn't quite right, because it was covering a rectangular structure rather than a circular one. But it had worked. There was no central pole, and the wooden rods all supported each other perfectly.

Celal had returned home now, and Adnan was perched on a rock near the kitchen. With his small frame and long, thin limbs, he looked vaguely arachnid. The air had turned decidedly cool, and I pulled a sweater on. Gone were the late evenings. It was barely 7:30pm but the sun was already setting. Autumn had arrived.

"I really don't think you can live in that tent all winter, Kerry." Adnan turned to the platform, his face puckered in concern. It was an opinion I kept hearing lately, and I was turning horribly stubborn about it.

"Of course I can! I love being in a tent – the sound of the birds, the smell of the forest. I hate walls!" I threw my hands up in disgust.

"But it's gonna get real cold. And when the evenings really pull in, what are you gonna do?"

"I shall worry about that when the time comes. I have an arctic sleeping bag. I'm sure I'll be fine."

Adnan peered up at me, the corners of his mouth releasing a fraternal grin. He scratched his chin, then his scalp.

"Okay, but if you need a place to shelter, you can stay at mine. I'm not gonna be here a lot of the winter. I've gotta get back to Afghanistan for a story."

Yes. That's what Adnan thought. But that was before he became embroiled in another more exciting adventure, one neither of us knew about at the time. Afghanistan would be but a skip in the park compared to the gut-wrenching trials and tribulations of something called "earthbag building".

As the light turned from copper to silver, the rocks shone in their soil beds. The dirt itself seemed to be breathing as the air above it cooled. Tree roots stretched underground drawing up water. Subterraneous fungal pathways glimmered with bio-chemical information. Earthworms tunnelled endlessly through the soil, while bugs crawled over the top. Humus degraded. Bacteria multiplied. The dirt was ready. And it was waiting.

Storm Coming

"Big wind coming. Big rain coming!" Dirt Woman ran out of the forest and across the land. The thick bands of her hamstrings flexed as she leaped over the earth. Her eyes shone like white eggs. She landed over by my hammock, grinning and whooping, and began rocking it like a deranged child.

"Exciting, eh?" I said.

"You no scared?"

"Nope. I can't wait. I've tied the tent to the platform so it can't blow away."

The day was only just hanging on to the coat-tails of afternoon. Evening skulked behind the mountain peaks. A sturdy wind was ushering it in on the swaying treetops, and it whooshed and swished as it approached. Cloud battalions had long cluttered the sky, and they were just beginning to march inland.

I scanned my dirt world. Having spent the entire day running around in a state of panic, my muscles now dragged with fatigue. But all seemed to be in its place. I'd stuffed as many possessions as I could inside my tent, and the sides bulged like canvas cheeks full of boiled sweets. My kitchen was another matter though. Glancing over at it – the dirt floor, the pots resting on rocks, the utensils hanging from the scraggy branches – I wondered how it would fare. Its only protection was Grandmother Olive.

"Winter coming. This first day."

Dirt Woman grabbed one of Grandmother Olive's lower branches with both hands, and walked her bare feet up the trunk. Then she hauled herself into the arms of this elegant tree. I sat sideways in my hammock. Then I pulled off my boots and socks, shivering in delight as the air rushed through my toes. Grabbing the edges of the hammock, I perched upright in it, using it like a garden swing.

"What do you do in winter? I mean, where do you go?" Arcing my head back I saw Dirt Woman crouched in the woody joint between trunk and bough, hugging her sun-scorched knees to her chest.

"I have cave. Beautiful cave. And on bad weather day, I go in there. Maybe I stay there many day."

"What do you do in there?"

"Winter very good time. Quiet time. I go there and listen Rock and Tree, and Pig and Bat. I talk with Owl and Fox, Snake and Ant. I listen their story and they listen my story. When I sit quiet many day, all the story mix in me."

"Wow. Like a big cooking pot?" I pointed to my open-air kitchen.

Dirt Woman nodded. "All the story get mix till they turn like very small seed."

I swung a little harder, my bare feet dragging through the layer of crisp, brown leaves on the dirt. "Okay. Like a distilled nugget of all the land's stories. Then what?"

And here my cave-dwelling sister smiled so wide and true, I just wanted to hug her. "I take seed from my head and put in my heart, and new dream story grow from it," she said.

I stopped swinging and dug my feet into the mulch. It was a thrilling concept, taking all the land's stories, cooking them up, and creating a new dream out of them.

"So everything has a story?" I threw the question up to my friend.

"What you think?" The dirt woman released her knees and dropped her legs either side of the branch. One grimy foot swung inches from my nose.

"I suppose yes, everything does. It's how we understand time. Past, present, future. Narrative is how we make sense of everything."

"And we must make beautiful story. Every year more beautiful."

Staring out onto my realm – the dusty stone ridge with my glorious little shed, and my $50 Carrefour tent tethered to its new platform, the forest behind it bucking and bending – I pondered on what she had said. "So what story seed did you plant last year then?" I asked.

The wind blew, and there was a patter as olives, twigs, and leaves flurried to the ground. Dirt Woman's face became animated, her eyebrows wriggling like a couple of thick centipedes. "Last year I want make very beautiful thing...Last year I have big dream. I want live in forest! I want be with tree and talk with all animal and bird. I want be *free*! Free for make more beautiful story."

I stared up at her nonplussed, feeling my features contorting into a bunch of confused shapes.

"But...but you always *were* free, weren't you? I mean, I thought you were already living in the forest."

Abruptly Dirt Woman jumped from her branch into my hammock. The whole thing lurched and swayed, the olive branches creaking in shock. She brought her face inches from mine, her eyes popping out like glistening black toadstools. "You no remember?" she said, cheekbones and brow rising in astonishment. I shook my head, not understanding what on Earth she was talking about."

"Before we here, we live in so bad and ugly place. There was no tree, and much wheel machine. I no smell the grass and all air was so dirty, so bad you cover mouth."

"You were there? You were in *Taiwan*?"

Dirt Woman stared at me. Her eyes were black galaxies now. As I stared into them I saw thousands of other worlds rolling and spinning like nuclei in inky cytoplasm. And the more I looked, the dizzier I felt, until I had no idea if I was inside her or out. The hammock creaked like an old rocking chair in front of a fire, while the wind bellowed and roared all around. Everywhere I could hear leaves swirling to the ground. It felt like the entire land was now a vortex with reality spinning away from its edges.

"Last year I make one more dream story." Dirt Woman was whispering now, her voice not much more than a husky murmur.

I blinked, trying to pull myself out of her disorienting gaze. But the centrifugal force was too compelling. "What else did you dream?" I asked, my throat contracting.

"I dream you see me and hear me," she said.

Bam! I snapped my eyes shut. But it was too late. The hammock was wobbling and swaying alarmingly with both of us in it, and all of a sudden I lost my grip on the edge. Before I could stop myself I toppled out and into the dirt. Laying there under the olive tree the dust whirling around me, I stared up stunned. Dirt Woman was stretched out in my hammock chuckling like a little finch.

The sharp edges of the world lost their definition as the squalls created small cyclones in the dust. A gust whipped Dirt Woman's dreadlocks, animating them until they rose like serpents from the clay of her head. Who was creating who here? Who was the real one?

Lying there, back and butt in the earth, I thought of all the times I'd escaped the mundane, all the times I'd left an old life that was dying and jumped into the new. And I just knew it had been Dirt Woman who had pushed me. Somewhere below the surface of my mind, I must have caught a few words of her calling. Somewhere in the depths of my psyche, I must have heard her stories. Her dreams.

The wind began to howl. The sky turned as grey as Neolithic slate. As the storm gathered itself on the threshold of the land, I began to roar with laughter. Then I sprang up out of the dirt and growled. Such an energy filled me, I was aflame. Bounding along the top of the land, I executed a surprisingly decent cartwheel. The forest was so close now, I could smell it. Night was drifting out from between the pine trunks, calling me home.

Sliding between the branches, I stalked into the woods. The leaves brushed over my bare skin like the sorcerer's fingers. The dry bracken tittered excitedly underfoot. My eyes rolled and my muscles sang as I wove deeper and deeper into the heart of the trees. How still it was in that arboreal Eden, the trees and shrubs forming a living refuge from the wind outside.

Soon I found the small old carob tree, the first that Dirt Woman had showed me. With her branches akimbo, she looked like a priestess giving rites. Sitting beneath her I dug myself into her roots hearing the canopy above churning like the surface of the sea. Soil covered my feet.

It was under my nails and in my hair. And as the dirt mixed with my sweat I sensed a type of ecstasy.

Dusk tipped into darkness, and slowly I rose and padded back to my tent. It was rippling and writhing like a tarp possessed. Opening the hatch, I fought my way inside, relishing the familiar smell of the kilim and canvas. As I pulled the rain cover down, I saw the forest ducking and diving as wind turned to gale. The pine needles whooshed and whistled. Such a happiness burst into my chest as I yanked down the zipper and pulled off my clothes.

I was safe. I was home. And I was a witch. But there was something that made me even happier. And that was that I was now a woman. Not some two-dimensional, perfumed and pretty, amenable tool of the mass media. Nor an emotionally stunted, intuition-starved, manservant of The System. No. I was real and alive. Pumped full of Earth magic. Straight from the dirt itself.

Grandmother Olive

Celal and his stone wall

Dudu (right) making bread with her family

My first proper structure: The shed

***

*If you enjoyed this book, please leave a review with
your online retailer, or with Goodreads.
It will be greatly appreciated.*

Acknowledgements

Nothing of any value happens as a result of one person. So many things and people contribute to a piece of work, including many I may not be aware of.

First, as always, a big thank you to my dad who always supports my schemes, no matter how hair-brained, and for offering me shelter in times of need. A thank you to Betty Rampling too for her input throughout.

Much gratitude goes to Emma Batchelor for her poetic insight, intelligent ideas, and her invaluable editorial contributions to this book. I am also much indebted to Sandi Berumen for her keen eye when reading the first draft, and for her ongoing support of my work. Many thanks also go to Dianne Güngör for her useful comments and contributions to the second draft.

Claire Raciborska's edit brought many new things to light. A big hug to her for helping tie up some important ends in a short amount of time.

Melissa Maples has been an online rock these past months. I'm so grateful for her reliability and overall competence, not to mention her superb photography. She has taken a sizeable technological weight off my shoulders.

Many thanks indeed to Catherine Stevenson for giving me permission to use her illustration in this book.

Thank you to Helen Baggott for her careful proofreading of the final draft.

This book has materialised thanks to the funding of everyone on Patreon, without which I would have had to give up *The Mud Home* website and the writing that goes with it. I am both humbled and motivated by the amount of backing I've received. Special thanks goes to Ewald and Micheala Derkits, Emma Winfield Tubb, Sam Creveling, and Greg Pappas for their generous and enduring support. It's been a pleasure to work with you. Many thanks also to Patti Delang, Susanne Feigum, Camilla MacDonald, Mary Silver, Nicodemus Ford, Terry L. McLain, Nanda Doornik,

Nick, Glena Sims Wright, Joel S. Henderson, Çiğdem Eldeleklioğlu, Thomas Adams, Jeanne Rucquoi from 3 Moons Project, Elaine Sheldon, Leila Dethelfsen, Torsten Meyer, Angela Clark, Catherine Guerra, Janet Whisnant, Patsy Anne Sawyer, Jas Cade, Donna Trimble, Alain Bidaine, Robert Macdonald, Ann Thijs, Jarbas M. Godoy Junior, Christina Massey, Darshana Maya Greenfield, William I. King Junior, Katie Duncan, Thomas Adams, Alison Lewin, Luisa Lyons, Simone Pettinger, Karuna Honer, Dora G. Robertson, Ian Quayle, Jan Zandvoort, Jacob Sour, Ruby Jan, Kit Springs, Tom Brennan, Sean Manners, Merete Bach-Pedersen, Philippa Rees, Kaliya Crowe, Judith Champion, Helen Breewood, Dimitar Marinov, Joyce Johnson, James Pietruszka, Ann Küçük, Funda Çılga, Cath Coffey, Rob Rogerson, Tom Andrews, Suzy Stone, Jim Zack, Mary de los Reyes, Yüsüf Akın Köksal, Jennifer Gill-Cronk, Lynn Peskoran, Leo Fischer, Bernadette Barrett, Natalie Jobanputra, Catherine Mary O'Shea, Jodie Harburt, Janet Hunter, Daniele Sumerix, Tamara Kuech, Maureen DA Rosa, Alexander Sofa, Erika Kretzmer, Noelie Bodin, Sally Steiner, Peter Farmer, Brigitte Muir, Anne Trim, Udo & Tere Schmidt, Christian De Leon-Horton, Violeta Domozina, Eva Scherer, Paul Lavallee, Tim Williams, Green Way of Life, Devta Singh, Alex King, Jerry Naughton, Ella Hall, Hugh Morshead, Mike Eaton, Jimmy Devenport, and Dee Brown.

Atulya K Bingham is a natural builder and author. Her other books include: 2014 OBBL winner *Ayse's Trail*, and her most popular book *Mud Ball*.

You can find a wealth of information on natural building and living off-grid at www.themudhome.com. If a deeper view of another way of life in nature you're after, you can follow her process of creating a new Eden in her *Earth Whispering* blog at:

www.themudhome.com/earthwhispering

The Next in This Series

'Kerry, we have a problem,' said Adnan.

I groaned. I was starting to feel like the ground control supervisor of Apollo 13. Where did all these damn problems keep sprouting from? They were like wayward eyebrow hairs. Was there no end to them? I turned to my neighbour. 'What now?' I snapped.

'I have no idea how we missed this. You guys were measuring with a plumb line when I was gone, right?'

'Of course!' I stood up indignantly. After the ubiquitous translation, Esra's eyes drew together outraged. *'Tabi ki!'* she said in Turkish, repeating exactly what I'd said.

'Well, I guess you weren't doing it, like top to bottom. Because if I let the plumb line drop from the top of *this* part of the wall...' And here Adnan climbed up on to our plank scaffold, then dropped the stone on the string that was our plumb line. 'You can see it's like...hell, Kerry! It's a good ten centimetres out! The front wall is *leaning*. Holy shit...this *can't* be good!'

I managed a good two minutes of stoicism before my self-control splintered. The definitive crack of my mood was probably heard as far as Dudu's house. I was simply too tired. Resting my head in my hands I pouted, suddenly feeling an irrational urge to locate a sledgehammer and start whacking slews out of the wall. As it happened, even if I had found a sledgehammer, the wall would have stayed standing. That's the way it is with earthbag roundhouses. I stood up and kicked the bag stand. After growling at the offending bulge for a minute or two, I plucked the tape measure from its nail in the shed. 'Alright, let's measure it!' I barked.

As humans are always more eager to learn of disaster than triumph, the team crowded round eagerly for a closer look. Esra was chewing her thumb while Adnan held the plumb line. I measured the distance from the base of the wall. It was near on 15 centimetres out. Sitting back on my heels I started to feel marginally persecuted. Obviously this was terrible. Walls are not made to lean. We needed a solution.

(Excerpt from *Mud Ball*)

"A joy from beginning to end – a brave, funny, moving account of building a new life and a new home out of mud in Turkey's mountain wilderness."
Sara Crowe, author of the acclaimed novel 'Bone Jack'.

The Mud Home